Justin Wilson's Cajun Humor

By

JUSTIN WILSON

and

HOWARD JACOBS

PELICAN PUBLISHING COMPANY
Gretna 1985

Library of Congress Cataloging in Publication Data

Wilson, Justin.
  Justin Wilson's Cajun Humor.
  1. Title: Cajun Humor.
PN6162.W54   818'.5'407   73—22164
ISBN: 0-88289-017-4 (Hardcover)
ISBN: 0-88289-317-3 (Paperback)

Manufactured in the United States of America

Designed by Oscar Richard

Published by Pelican Publishing Company, Inc.
630 Burmaster Street, Gretna, Louisiana 70053

Introduction

Everything about Justin Wilson is prodigious—his bacchanalian appetite, his boundless enthusiasm and unquenchable sense of humor, his inexhaustible fund of stories and his vast reservoir of mouth-induced sound effects. And, finally, his passion for the comforts and luxuries of life ("Either go first class or go home, you year?").

I well remember a luncheon engagement with this gifted Cajun talespinner, and we were to meet in the lobby of the Monteleone Hotel in New Orleans. But we found the restaurant crowded. "I don't like dis some a-tall," groused Wilson, lapsing into the Cajun patois with which he is so closely identified.

So he approached the room clerk and, in that musically resonant voice of his, instructed the greeter to "gimme de bes' suits in de house dair." Escorted by the bemused bellhop, we took the "allegator" to the 12th floor, where we were ceremoniously ushered into a luxury suite. There, after a scrumptious dinner, we discussed details of this volume for a couple of hours, then checked out.

I never knew whether this "bes' suits in de house" was complimentary, or whether the tariff came from Wilson's own pocket. I didn't care to know, because if the latter were the case I was a likely candidate for an "apologetic stroking," to use his own terminology.

On another occasion I had breakfast with the leonine-headed humorist in the Fairmont, and there his gargantuan appetite surfaced. He ordered a breakfast steak, two stacks of buttered toast, a double orange juice, six strips of bacon and four eggs. When I expressed astonishment that anybody could consume four fried eggs after the other heaping dishes, he replied, "I got to pass an apologize, me. If I wasn't off my feed, I would order six eggs."

They tell the story that two of his fellow-townsmen were discussing Wilson and one observed, "You know, Juice-tanh has got an appetite as big as all outdoors." "Yeah," replied the other, "and he'd eat dat too if dey could got it to de table."

His massive reservoir of Cajun tales is distinguished not only by the snap, crackle and pop of his punchlines, but also by the little personal touches he adds as he goes along. I once remarked to one of his innumerable "frien's" that Wilson was unquestionably one of the greatest embellishers I had ever met. "You don't mean to tole me," exclaimed the frien'. "Au' I never t'ought he aver stole a nickel in his life."

The locale of most of Wilson's rollicking yarns is bucolic, deep in the Teche country of South Louisiana. Occasionally he allows some of his frien's to go North—to Shreveport. But they are most comfortable in their natural habitat of moss-draped oaks and bayous and pirogues and sauce piquante, licking pot hounds, A-Model T Fords and country Cadillacs—or picking up trucks.

A master of the king's English, Wilson in character doesn't speak as conventional folk do. In the bayou society in which he and his frien's move, nobody has a first or last name, but rather a front name and behind name. His characters "granulate" from college, they don't get disheartened at setbacks, but "lose dey discourage, plumb." They rarely "look at" an object, especially a beautiful one, but admiringly "cass an' eye" on it. His waitresses are not merely waitresses, but female lady womans waitresses, and they seldom go anywhere, when they can just as easily "pass ma'se'f by."

Wilson doesn't boast about his distinguished forebears, and if you remark that he sprang from a long line of peers, he will say deprecatingly, "I don't know about dat, but I did jomp off a couple of docks, I ga-ron-tee."

He glides effortlessly from one story to another with a casual "You know, lady an' gentlemans," or "I got a frien'," or "I never will fo'got." Most of his stories do, in fact, involve the didoes of his innumerable "frien's," although Wilson himself occasionally is the protagonist of the droll tales.

As in the lusty western towns of the 19th century, many of Wilson's anecdotes revolve about, or originate in, or are related in, the town tavern, or "barroom saloon," as he redundantly calls it. To hear him tell it, he never wets his whistle with anything stronger than buttermilk in these rustic ginmills, and nobody ever patronizes one except to hold a meeting—presumably of the church sociable variety. Which makes it all the more surprising that some of his tee-totaler characters manage to get themselves "dronk, an' good!"

The Wilson anecdotes can be broadly classified into two main categories. The first embodies tales of pure fantasy, so far-fetched they admittedly could not have happened without supernatural intervention. Yarns about talking animals, for example, fall into this grouping.

7

In the second category are stories that could have happened with the aid of a little natural phenomena. And of course if they are punctuated by a resounding "I ga-ron-tee" the skeptic can no longer doubt their authenticity.

The plausible tales, as in any ideal Cajun story, concern themselves with the overflowing granaries of anecdotes involving Cajun names, the early settler's rampant misuse of words, his chucklesome misunderstanding of the question, his genius at leaping to conclusions, his language difficulty in giving directions, his superstition, his astuteness and the bizarre situations in which he ofttimes finds himself.

That booming "I ga-ron-tee!" uttered to place the final stamp of credibility on his tall tales, carries such soaring conviction as to suggest that it was underwritten jointly by the Bank of England and Chase Manhattan. His duck calls, sounded without benefit of any reed or other device and emitted solely with the aid of cupped hands, have lured colonies of mallard to their deaths, and have had a similar effect on many titillated listeners who have literally died laughing.

His version of a flat tire galumphing down the street, "buggety, buggety, buggety . . ." is so authentic as to suggest flat tires generally could take a few pointers from the rendition.

This Schiaparelli of humor can take a twice-told tale and so adorn it with verbal buttons and bows that often its own creator wouldn't recognize it. The difference between the raw and the finished product might be likened to a virgin pine before and after its metamorphosis into a dazzling Christmas tree. Wilson adorns it with malapropian ornaments ("De police petroleum car wit' de syringe on full blas' "), a few garlands of metaphor and simile ("She snuggled up to him like a sick kitten to a hot rock"), tinsel of expletives ("I'd hate like hell to be a Cajun from Hyannisport, I garon-tee!"), and a few sprigs of orgiastic exclamations, such as WHOO BOY!

His SHOOM is the closest thing to greased lightning since the heyday of Speedy Gonzales.

Once his tale is completed, there emerges a splendiferous tree whose vocal equivalent has enabled Wilson to keep his listeners eating out of his hand via lectures and recordings for many years.

As the reader runs the rapids of Wilson's choice yarns, he will see that Cajun humor is basically kindly, often quixotic and rarely biting or sarcastic or morbid, as are many stories perpetrated on television or the night club circuit.

Justin Wilson's voracious appetite eminently qualifies him as a gourmand, and he is also a peerless chef whose fund of mouth-watering recipes is virtually limitless. But viewing his television series on the preparation of scrumptious dishes, one must take with a grain of salt the quantities of wine, condiments and spices he recommends. For while this is Cajun-style cookery at its best, it is also the most pungent. Wilson is in truth a man for all seasonings, and it is commonplace for him to prescribe a pinch of cayenne pepper while sprinkling it about his concoction of the moment as liberally as though it was going out of style.

A product of the lush agricultural country, Wilson speaks affectionately of his birthplace of Amite, Louisiana, just a whoop and a holler from New Or—lee—anh, which is also the locale of numerous Wilson anecdotes. His nonagenarian mother, Mrs. Harry D. Wilson, is a grande dame of the old school and the widow of Harry D. Wilson, for 32 years the Louisiana state commissioner of agriculture, or, as his son would put it, "commissioner of adgi−culture." Two of his three sisters, Mrs. Guy Garrison and Mrs. Bolivar E. Kemp, Jr., still reside, as does their mother, in Amite, a history−steeped community where columned homes of another era rise in stately contrast to the no−nonsense efficiency of modern construction. His third sister, Mrs. Roy Heidelberg, makes her home in Covington, deep in the piney woods of Southeast Louisiana.

Wilson himself, and his charming helpmeet, Sara, reside near Denham Springs, just outside the state capital of Baton Rouge. From his comfortable diggings in the countryside he fans out into all corners of the "U. S. an' A" to joust with appreciative audiences and agitate their collective funnybone while eliminating their ignorance of Cajun manners, customs and patois. Many of his forays are free of sponsorship except by the group or organization which engages his services. In others he represents the state highway department, for which he has long been a consultant to, and lecturer on, highway safety.

His proudest recollection is of a meeting with the immortal Will Rogers that marked the turning point in his theretofore checkered career. As a young man, discouraged by the lukewarm reception accorded his foray into the field of humor, he had the good fortune to meet Rogers, to whom he confided his frustrations and disillusionment. To which the happy philosopher and humorist, almost on the eve of his ill−omened flight with Wiley Post, advised him vehemently, "You have the God−given ability to make people laugh, and you should never abandon it."

Thus inspired, Wilson went on to achieve an enviable reputation as a yarn−spinner in the Cajun manner. In the intervening 40 years he has appeared before audiences throughout the nation and, chuckle for

10

chuckle, has probably evoked as many belly laughs as any other humorist extant.

"The mainest t'ing in life is to make peoples laugh," he tells his audiences. Then he proceeds to do just that from the rostrum and via recordings, as well as through his most recent outlet, a televised Cajun cooking show.

What follows is basically the Justin Wilson brand of humor, told in his own effervescent style. It establishes what many of his admirers have always sensed—that here is a hedonist of the first water, reflecting in every word, action and gesture the typical Cajun zest for life and the keen enjoyment he derives therefrom.

As for the dialect, he uses that expertly as a setting and framework for the droll ideas, attitudes, culture and situations that he espouses. He is the first to admit that the patois is diminishing—an inevitable casualty of the proliferation of television, newspapers, railroads, highways and airlines of the past half century. The early French—speaking pioneers, struggling with the nuances of the English language, are gone, as are their first and second generation descendants who clung to the soil and the language of their hardy forebears. But succeeding generations, availing themselves of the burgeoning opportunities for education and worldly wisdom, abandoned the isolated towns and settlements in which their ancestors have lived out their lives. Capitalizing on their great vitality, natural intelligence and thirst for knowledge, they threw off any lingual deficiencies to which they might have been exposed. Today business and professional men of Cajun origin speak virtually flawless English, tinged only by the unmistakable Cajun accent which many retain for all their lives.

Nor has the native joie de vivre of the true Cajun ever forsaken him, and no one is better qualified than Justin Wilson to tell the world about it.

While yarns in the Wilson repertoire can be depended upon to produce laughter wherever they are told, the reaction is sometimes unpredictable, even to him. One would assume that the Cajun spelling of "Fido" as "Phideaux" would be the last word on the matter. But not so. A French scholar pointed out that, if one were going to maintain the fidelity of phonetic French, he would have to spell it "Failledeaux."

Wilson's opening remarks to his audiences invariably trace the origins and history of the prolific Cajuns, whose few thousands driven from Acadia in Nova Scotia have swollen to perhaps a million. The initial concentration in South Central Louisiana has spilled over into adjacent Texas and to the Mississippi Gulf Coast, while uncounted tens of thousands have migrated into every state of the union.

In appearance, Wilson cuts an imposing figure. Standing six feet, one inch and fluctuating the scales at a healthy 230 pounds, he has a cockatoo crest of steely grey hair and a bristling mustache always impeccably coiffed. He navigates with the aid of a cane, the result of an automobile accident that laid him low many years ago. But his stature is upright and vigorous, and he employs the cane with greatest eclat.

Our storyteller enacts the role of a knowledgeable Cajun of great savoir faire whose grammar might be wanting, but whose flair for whimsy and fantasy is unexcelled. His trademark is the customary absence of a coat, and the presence of a string tie and a pair of flaming red suspenders over a snow—white shirt. A flop-brimmed buff Panama hat usually adorns his head.

Wilson's explosive "How y'all are?" to an expectant audience is redolent of cordiality and likely to convert any initial antipathy or indifference on the part of his listeners to a mood of relaxed anticipation. And the

12

"behind" part of his signature, "I'm glad fo' you to see me, I ga—ron—tee," can be depended upon to shatter any lingering *tales* resistance.

Despite all the thousands of rollicking yarns that have spewed from the Wilson larynx, he has never heretofore transformed the spoken into the written word, except for a cookbook in which his recipes are the dominant theme and Cajun patois is infrequent. This, then, represents the first serious effort to commit to paper the choicest of his Cajun stories, complete with inflections, malapropisms and colloquialisms with which they abound.

HOWARD JACOBS

Conversion Specialist

Howard Jacobs' part in the creation of this volume was to write the story captions and the Introduction and to select and convert Wilson's rib-tickling anecdotes from the spoken into the written word.

Over the years as a veteran and widely read author-columnist for the New Orleans *Times-Picayune,* Jacobs has exhibited a keen appreciation of, and sensitivity to, dialect. This is particularly true in the Cajun milieu, in which he has acquired a high proficiency. His book-length magazine feature *Cajun Laugh-In,* acclaimed as the first serious effort to get Cajun patois onto paper, inspired talespinner Wilson to approach the columnist with a suggestion that they collaborate on a book of Wilson's stories. A year in the making, *Justin Wilson's Cajun Humor* was the result.

A native of Lake Charles, Louisiana, and resident of New Orleans since adolescence, Jacobs has flourished on the east and west peripheries of Cajunland all his life, and his exposure to the Cajun dialect and way of life has been extensive and continuous. Hundreds of Cajun stories, many of them credited to Justin Wilson, have appeared in his daily column "Remoulade" since its inception in 1948.

Jacobs' most recent book, *Charlie the Mole and Other Droll Souls,* is a collection of stories about

whimsical and offbeat citizens who have flashed across
the New Orleans horizon for the past three decades.

The Cajun Patois

Would you like to be an instant Cajun? Then take a cram course in the colorful Cajun patois, Justin Wilson style. First off, you convert as many words as possible, especially multiple—syllable words, into other words. Care must be taken that the substitution sounds phonetically similar to the original, but conjures up an entirely different image. In the Wilson ossified glossary, a man who sells real estate is a real astute salesman. And a customer who buys on time often purchases on the lay—awake plan. This is a happy conversion, as any debtor will attest who has lain awake brooding as to how he was going to meet the next installment.

Add as many "ings" to the adjective in a compound word as the traffic will bear, such as "roughin'neck or draftin' board" for "roughneck" or "draft board." And see to it that your characters don't suffer an ordinary apoplectic stroke when they can just as well have an apologetic stroking. Take yourself real serial, and every time you return from a duck hunt you clean your twice-barrell Caribbean or your ah—romatic shoot gun.

Put your verbs in the past tense, wherever feasible. Example: "I'm gonna tole you." Don't ever "go" anywhere, but "brought you'se'f" and "pass you'se'f by." Always substitute "once" for "one," or "twice" for "two," to achieve some ludicrous constructions. "World War Twice" is far more likely to evoke laughter than is "World War Two."

Try changing your nouns to verbs, even if you have to make your verb plural. Surely Wilson's "Dass where de imagines come in" is preferable to the commonplace "Dass where de imagination comes in." And if you're tempted to use a word like "taboo," don't. Just emulate Wilson's eloquent "I've got de prohibits." And such descriptive adjectives as "wondermous" and "pitimous" have got "wonderful" and "pitiful" beat all hollow when it comes to a matter of vivid description. And always remember, in order to have a good time you have to "pass pleas—zure" in the Cajun vernacular. Once you "pass pleas—zure," then you're "gettin'you' enjoys."

Final letters in many words are dropped for perfect Wilsonia. Thus "your" would emerge as "you'," "and" as "an'," and "with" as "wit'." Sometimes, for the purposes of clarity, it is necessary to retain the final letter. Since "door" might be misinterpreted if written as "do'," it is usually spelled in full, and sometimes so are similar words such as "more" or "four."

Wilson's frien's rarely have an argument, but an "argue." And "instructions" become "instructs," such as "Read de instructs . . . "

Verb tenses are ofttimes changed in this never—never land of fractured English. A cooking turkey, or chicken, for example, is seldom "done." Invariably it comes out "did," as "I t'ink de shicken is did."

Drop your h's following the letter "t" in many nouns, so that "things" become "t'ings," while the dipthong "th" in articles and pronouns usually emerges with the "d" sound ("de," "dem," "dose," "dat" and the like). Convert the plural to singular, and vice—versa, such as "dat mans on de levee," or "lady an' gentlemans."

Preface any sentence involving your own opinion, intent or suggestion with a "me," and conclude it, where stress is needed, with a vigorous "yeah" or "no." Example: "Me, I'm goin' to town, yeah!" Or, "Don't hit me in ma' look wit' dat wet mop, no!"

Whenever possible, employ some part of that object or thing to identify the entire object. For instance, "One ma' good frien's live down de gravel apiece from me."

Master these grammatical deviations, and the result is instant Cajun patois, Justin Wilson style.

Justin Wilson's Cajun Humor

Half-Bleed Cajun

How y'all are? I'm glad fo' you to see me, I ga—ron—tee. But no matter how smaht you may be, or w'at you may do, some of you may not know w'at a Cajun is—an' I don't want any of you to leave here 'til I cure you of dat failin' fault.

I'm goin' to axplain to you 'zactly w'at a Lewisana Cajun is. Now me, I'm jus' half—bleed, I'm not full—bleed. Sometime I wish I was full-bleed, but iss a damm good t'ing I'm not, 'cause I can't stood a full dose o' dis. Now C—a—j—u—n is usually de way iss spelled. Iss a mutilation of de word "Acadian." Acadia was a small section of Nova Scotia where a group of peoples had come dair from France an' lived dair happily. Dey had freedom of axpression, freedom of religion an' de pursuit of happiness. An' 218 years ago dese peoples who had come to Acadia—or as we say in French, "Ah—cah—dee"—lan' in dair from France, England took over. In dose days England was subjec' to doin' dat—befo' she became a welfare state. An' de English tole all dose French peoples who lived dair an' spoke nuthin' but French becaus' dey were French, say, "Look, you got to swear allegiance to de King o' England." But dey would not did dat—dey would jus' swear at 'im, an' real good.

So de English tole dem peoples, "Look, you got to leave here," an' dey would not did dat too. So dey ran 'em down an' let 'em carry all dat dey could in two arm—dat is, all dey could catch. Dey put dem on small sailin' vessels an' dey come down de Atlantic seacoas' comin' to Lewisana where some o' dem had frien's or relatives an' dey knew some odder peoples down here.

Now history has it dat dey tried to lan' in New England, an' dem good, church—goin' peoples wouldn't let 'em. An' I certinly am glad. I'd hate like hell to be a Cajun from Hyannisport, I ga—ron—tee.

So dey came on down, an' soon landed in Maryland an' Virginia an' Nort' Carolina an' Georgia. But most of 'em were coming for Lewisana. Dey had some pretty poor navigators, an' some o' dose boats landed in Alabama an' some in Mississippi—an' a couple o' blind toms hit Taxes.

But de majority o' dem went into avery bay an' river mout' in de Golf of Mexico an' scattered t'ruout Sout' Lewisana. Now in French you pronounce de word "Acadian" "Ah—cahd—ee—onh," or "Ah—cahd—ee—anh," dependin' on what kind of Ah—cahd—ee—onh or Ah—cahd—ee—anh you may be. An' in Sout' Lewisana, an Acadian bein' a true Southerner, dey became Kah-jonh, or Kah-janh, pronounce in Spanish "Ca—hoon." An' dass axactly what a Cajun is.

Under the Influence

Years ago I had a good frien' w'at had been up Nort'—aroun' Shreveport—an' he was drivin' up an' down dem deep hill between here an' Shongaloo w'en he hit a rut an' turn his car over eight or saven time. A fallow wit' a blue coat an' brass button—one dem policeman cop—pull him out de wreckage an' stan' dat li'l Cajun up an' say, "Are you dronk?"

"Hell, yeah," he say. "You don't t'ought I'm one dem reckless driver, hanh?"

Turncoat

In Worl' War Twice I never will fo'got I was in Kaplan nine mile wes' of a li'l town name Abbeville, Lewisana. A whole bunch of us were in a barroom saloon havin' a meetin'—drinkin' buttermilk. An' a Cajun came runnin' in an' say, "We got to leave here r'at now. I jus' heard on de ray—dio dat de German was all over Abbeville. Les get goin'."

"Wait jus' a minute," I tol' him. "Dat's not Abbeville, Lewisana no. Dass Abbeville, France, w'at Abbeville, Lewisana, was name after."

Oh," averybody say wit' big relief. An' dey sat deyse'f back down an' start de meetin' over ag'in.

"I feel so sorry fo' dem Franchman I don't know w'at to did," one dem fallow say.

"Not me," anudder fallow say. "I ain' got a damm bit o' sympathize fo' 'em. Dey never should a lef' Lewisana an' gone over dair in de firs' place."

Curiosity Bump

You know, dey got dis fallow all de time ax 'is teacher, "How come?" How come dis, how come dat, how come dis, an' his teacher got so damm tired of it she didn't know w'at to did. So she say like dis, "Don't say 'how come.' Say 'why.'"

An' dat fallow say, "How come why?"

25

Reincarnation

De Dixon an' Mason line run r'at t'rough Bunkie, an' anyt'ing nort' of dat is damyankees as far as us Cajun is concern. I never will fo'got, dis frien' wit' me was in one dem barroom saloon—dronk, I mean! So he brought hisse'f out dat barroom saloon an' he suspose to took a r'at han' an' brought hisse'f home. But he don't did dat. He took a lef' han' into a cemetery—how you call grave—YARD. But it been rain' fo' or t'ree day, an' averyt'ing wet an' slickery, I mean! An' he come to one dem open grave an' he haul off—KERPLOOM—an' fall in dair. At firs' he try to clam' hisse'f out, but iss slickery, an' he dronk, an' dat don't halp some a—tall. So he start yellin' "He'p me, I'm cold! He'p me, I'm cold!"

After a li'l while one his frien' brought hisse'f out o' dat barroom saloon in de same shape like him—dronk. But he got a big cur—ous, like all us Cajun, an' w'en he hear dat "He'p me, I'm cold. He'p me, I'm cold!" he got to go see w'at dat is. So he follow de soun' till he brought hisse'f r'at up to dat grave, an' he look down an' dat odder fallow is lyin, dair shoutin' "He'p me, I'm cold. He'p me, I'm cold!" De fallow stoodin' dair say, "Of cou'se you cold. You done kick off all you' dirt!"

Advanced Stage

In World War Twice a bunch of us went to Camp Beauregard in Alexandria. Dat's where dey induce you. I remember dey put one man in charge, an' dass de meanes' man I never saw befo' again in ma' life. He

26

worked us from befo' daylight 'til plum'—till we was plum' wore out. One dem fallow come to me an' say, "Juice-tanh, how come dey put dat mean so—an'—so in charge of us, hanh?"

I say, "Becaus' dat mans had ROTC befo' he brought hisse'f into de sarvice."

He say, "WHOO! He mus' got it damm bad, I ga—ron—tee!"

Last Straw

I got a frien' w'at got a li'l boy chirren not quite savan, an' up to de time he not quite savan he don' said a word. An' his ma—ma an' pa—pa dey worry, hoo manh, you KNOW. So dey took dat li'l boy chirren to de doc—taire an' he look him over an' say, "He hokay physical. Mebbe up dair (an' he hit his head), but you better brought him home an' see w'at happen."

Den one day at breakfas' dat li'l fallow say, "Ma—ma, dis toas' is burn like de devil, I ga—ron—tee." Well, his ma—ma do a handsprung r'at now, an' his pa—pa los' his spoke plumb, he so sopprise. Den his ma—ma say, "Son, how come you don' say nothin' an' den you say somet'ing after all dese year?"

An' dat li'l boy chirren say, "Up to now, averyt'ing been hokay!"

Retarded Canine

You know, down in Sout' Lewisana all us Cajun like to hont, an' mo' pa'tic—lar we like to hont dem dock, I ga—ron—tee. I got a frien' w'at is not de bes' in de worl' an' de U. S. an' A, he's de vary bes'. An' averybody ax him, "How 'bout takin' me hontin' wit' you'?" An' he always say "No," an' sometime, "HELL NO."

One day one dem banking peoples say, "Ma' frien', I would like you to take me wit' you to hont some dock," an' ma' frien' say, "No." Den dat banking peoples w'at had loan him some money on his house say, "You like dat house I loan you some money on, hanh?" Now you don' got to hit my frien' in de face wit' a wet mop, an' he say, "Hokay, brought you' pickin' up truck an' got me at fo' t'irty a.m. in de mornin'."

So dat banking peoples come by, an' w'en ma' frien' come out de banking peoples say, "Where's Phideaux?" An' ma' frien' say, "We don' need Phideaux." An' dat banking peoples say, "Brought de dorg an' don' gimme some argue. So ma' frien' call Phideaux, an' he jomp in de pickin' up truck-KERPLOOM.

After ma' frien' an' de banking peoples got in a pirogue boat, ma' frien' use his dock call—QUANH, QUANH, QUANH, QUANH, QUANH. An' here come a dock in a bunch all by hisse'f. De banking peoples point his ah—romatic shootgun, BLOOM, an' dat dock fall r'at in de water. De banking peoples say, "Send Phideaux to got de dock," an' ma' frien' say, "We don' need to. Dat dock ain' goin' nowhere." An' de banking peoples say, "Sen' Phideaux to got de dock an' don' gimme some argue."

So ma' frien' say, "Hokay, go got de dock, Phideaux," an dat dorg goes trip, trip, trip, trip, r'at on top de water an' brought dat dock back in de boat. De banking peoples don' say a word.

Den ma' frien' calls anudder dock all in a bunch by hisse'f, raise his twice—barrel Caribbean an' KERPLOOM, an' dat dock go down like a rock. An' he say, "Phideaux, go got dat dock," an' Phideaux goes trip, trip, trip, trip, trip, r'at on top de water an' brought dat dock back to de boat.

"You know," dat banking peoples say, "I didn' say nothin' de firs' time because I t'ought it was a damn lie. But did you see dat dorg walk on top de water twice, hanh?"

"Yes," ma' frien' say, "an' it embarrass me more den I can say. You know, I never could taught dat dorg to swim!"

Horrible Example

I got a frien' who's rich—WHOO, manh, you jus' don' know. One day he brought hisse'f to New Or—lee—anh an' go to one dem hotel, where he got a whole suits. Den he called a bellman boy name LaGrange from Opelousas, an' he say, "I want a female womans." An' LaGrange say, "You got de r'at man, I ga—ron—tee. W'at you want, blonde brunette, chatain, redhead?" An' ma' frien' say, "She got to be a special kind o' female womans. She got to be a redhead." "I can got dat," LaGrange say. "An' she got to be six foots, fo' inch tall an' weigh 75 pound."

"What you said?"

"She got to be six foots, fo' inch tall an' weigh 75 pound."

"I don't t'ought I can fine one to meet dat specify," LaGrange say.

Ma' frien' reach in his pock—ett an' pro—duce a $50 bill, which he tore in half an' give one-half to LaGrange.

"Now brought me dat female womans," he say, "an' I'll give you de odder half. So got you'se'f los'! An' SHOOM, LaGrange was gone.

Half hour later he telephoned de suits. "I got a female womans," he say. "She don't 'zactly meet dem specify, but OOH MANH, sho close! She's a redhead, jus' like you ax. But she's only six foots, t'ree an' t'ree quarter inch, an' she weigh 78 poun'."

"Brought her up here an' lemme cass an eye on dat," ma' frien' say.

Soon dair was a knock on de do', an' stoodin' dair was de redhead wit' LaGrange behin'.

Ma' frien' cass jus' one eye on dat female womans. "Dass close enuf," he say, an' he han' de odder ha'f de 50−dollar bill to LaGrange. "Now got you'se'f los'," he say, an' SHOOM, LaGrange was disappear.

"Now," he say to dat female womans, "brought you'se'f in de middle de flo' an' took off all you' clothes—an' r'at now!"

SHOOM, she took off all her clothes.

Den ma' frien' brought hisse'f to de do' of de odder room in de suits an' open it. On de odder side was stoodin' his six-year-ol' redhead daughter, Celestine, cute li'l t'ing.

"You see dat?" he say, pointin' to de female womans. "Yeah pa−pa."

"Well, dass de way you gonna look if you don't drink you' milk, I ga−ron−tee!"

Reformed Pointer

I know a fallow who rich, manh, his oil wells can pump mo' money in one night den he can spen' de nex' day—an' dass rich! De Cajun believe money is somet'ing you spen' jus' befo' you got it, you know. An' de reason we feel like dat is dat we ain' never seen an armored car in a funeral pro—cession in our life. Well, one day dis fallow come to de clob where all us sports would hang aroun' an' shoot some pool.

An' he say to me like dis, "Juice-tanh, whass all dis pointin' dorg people talk about? W'at dat is, hanh?"

"Well," I say, "dass a dorg w'at fine de bird fo' you, an' w'en you shoot dat he go brought de bird back."

"You don't say! All I got is some lickin' pot hound, but no pointin' dorg. You can wrote a letter to a frien' w'at you got to sell me one dem t'ing?"

"But fo' sho'," I tol' him. So I give him a note to ma' frien' an' he brought hisse'f to see him. "Juice-tanh tol' me you got some good pointin' dorg," he say. "Me, I got to got one dem t'ing. Money ain' no ob-jec wit' me."

"Money ain' no ob-jec wit' me too," de manh say. "I don' ob—jec to it a-tall. Now you see dat dorg over dair? He one of de fines' in de worl'."

"He don' look so hot to me," dat fallow say. "I can see avery rib from r'at chere."

Now dem dorg fancy peoples, you can talk about dey wife an' dey chirren, but don' you talk about dey dorg, you year?" An' de manh say, "Look, you can bought de dorg or not bought him, but don' you talk about him!"

"I didn' mean to 'fence you none," dat fallow say.

"Hokay," de dorg fancy peoples say. "Now you took dat dorg out an' see how you like him."

So he was gone wit' de dorg fo' fo' or t'ree hour befo' he brought hisse'f back.

"How you like dat dorg?" de dorg fancy peoples say.

"Oh, dass a great dorg. Dass a fine dorg, dass a sweet dorg. Dass a wondermous dorg. But you know, w'en we started out dat dorg would come to a dead still like he put his immer—gency broke on, an' raise his front paw wit' his tail out stiff. An' I would yell, holler, whistle

31

an' scream, but dat dorg wouldn' budge hisse'f. But after I beat him fo' or t'ree time, I cured him o' dat habit, I ga—ron—tee!"

Obstacle Course

Dey got two fallow in Rayne in de Golden Peasant Cocktail Loonge. Dass on Highway 90, how—you—call de Old Spaniel Trail. Well, dey got so dronk dey can't clam' down from dem stool, an' dass bad, you year? Finally dey unclam' deyse'ves an' got down on dey han's an' knees an' walk out. On de odder side of de Old Spaniel Trail is de Sodden Pacific Railroad track, an' dem fallow start walkin' on de track.

"You know," one say, "Dass de longess' set of stairs anywhere in de worl', I ga—ron—tee."

"I don't mine de stairs so much," de secon' say, "but dem low han'rail is givin' me de devil."

Voracious Appetite

You know, not long ago dair was a ma—ma crawfish w'at took her li'l babies out to see de worl'. Dey had not gone but about t'irty feets w'en SHOOM, de li'l crawfish back up fas' to dey ma—ma. "Ma—ma," dey say, "w'at dat is hanh?"

"Don' be scared fo' dat, chirren," she say, "Dass a cow, an' a cow don' eat crawfish. Come on, le's go!"

Soon de baby crawfish t'row up dem claw an' SHOOM, double gear reverse. "What dat is, ma—ma? What dat big animals is, hanh?"

"Don' be scared fo' dat, chirren," de ma—ma say. "Dass a horse, an' a horse don' eat crawfish. Come on, le's go. I got to show you de worl' befo' dark."

Dey walk about t'irty t'ree mo' feets ag'in an' de ol' ma—ma crawfish t'row up bot' dem claw an' SHOOM, double high gear reverse. An' de li'l baby crawfish say, "W'at de matter, ma—ma, what de matter?"

She say, "You see dat ani-mule up dere, hanh?"

"Yeah, ma—ma."

She say, "Run like hell. Dass a Cajun, an' he'll eat any damm t'ing!"

Confused Motorist

We got a town down in Sout' Lewisana how—you—call Loff—i—yette. De engineer w'at laid Loff—i—yette out was dronk eight week befo' he drew de firs' line. Iss de only town in de U. S. an' A. where you can get los' in one block.

I never will forgot, de firs' time I brought ma'se'f to Loff—i—yette I was so los' I didn't know where I was los' from, an' dass bad, you year? Soon I come to a crossin' road I later foun' out was name Four Corner. I cas' an eye on a li'l boy stoodin' dair an' I brought my car to a dead still.

Den I say, "Son, brought you'se'f here, I wanna ax you somet'ing."

He say, "W'at dat is?"

"You can tole me where dis road on de r'at han' will took me if I got on dat, hanh?"

"Mister, I hate to tole you, but me, I don't know."

"How 'bout dis road on de lef', hanh? Can you tole me where dat road will took me if I got on dat?"

"Ag'in I hate to tole you, but me, I don't know dat too, no."

"How 'bout dat road straight ahead like I'm look? Can you tole me where dis road will took me if I stayed jus' like dat, hanh?"

"It broke ma' heart to tole you dis, but me, I don' know dat too, no."

"Son, I ain't gonna did it, but s'pose I turn ma'se'f aroun' an' go jus' like I come from. Can you tole me where dat road would took me if I dues dat, hanh?"

"On de groun' my heart is in a milyun li'l bitty pieces, iss broke so bad. But me, I don't know dat also too besides."

"Son, you don't know a damm t'ing."

"Dass r'at, but I ain't los', no!"

Sweet Revenge

Dey get dis fallow w'at live way down in a li'l town in Sout'wes' Lewisana name Rayne. One day he brough hisse'f to town an' he got a great big pack—age tie on his ches'. An' I ax him, I say, "W'at dat is you got tie on you' ches', hanh?"

He say, "Dynamite."

"W'at in de worl' you dues wit' dynamite tie on you' ches'?"

He say, "You know Emile Boudreaux?"

"Oh, hell yeah. I know dat Cajun, an' good."

Well, avery time I brought ma'se'f to town he walk up to me an' WHAM hit me in de ches' like dat an' broke avery see—gar w'at I got in ma' pock—ett. An' me, I'm gonna blow his doggone han' off, I ga—ron—tee!"

Diplomatic Empire

You know, lady an' gentlemans, down in Sout' Lewisana we used to have a bessball league call de Evangeline Bessball League. An' w'en dey start dat league back in de late 'Twenties an' early 'T'irties it was know as de Hot Pepper League, an' dass jus' w'at it was.

Dem Cajun took dat bessball real serial, I ga—ron—tee. An' dey would bet dey wife an' dey house an' dey chirren on an ordinary game. An' w'en dey got dat t'ing how—you—call playoff, WHOO MANH, dey'd bet dey house an' dey wife an' dey chirren an' dey crawlin' tractor an' dey T—model A Ford an' dey schicken an' dey dorg—averyt'ing w'at dey got.

An' I never will fo'got, Rayne an' Loff—i—yette got to play de playoff, an' Rayne won one game an' Loff—i—yette won one—tie, tie. So dey go to Rayne fo' de t'ird game an' Rayne make one run an' Loff—i—yette come r'at back wit' one run—tie, tie summore—one game apiece each, one run apiece each. Tight—OOH MANH!

An' Rayne was at bat an' Loff—i—yette in de fiel' an' de fallow at bat fo' Rayne was a great big mans, six foots, fo' inch, bat lef' han', weigh 130 pounds.

De catchin' man from Loff—i—yette w'at catch de ball de pitchin' man chunk is anodder big mans—six foots, five inch, wiegh 135 pound.

An' de empire, you know, dat mans w'at call de ball an' stan' behin' de pitchin' man . . . he weigh 90 pound soppin' wet wit' sweat an' 12 bottle wit' foam on top inside.

De count on de mans from Rayne is one strike an' one ball—tie, tie sommore. WHOO, iss tight, you know! An' de pitchin' man fo' Loff—i—yette SHOOM, he groove one by de corner o' dat plate.

35

De li'l empire put bot' han's behin' him an' back up fo' or t'ree feets an' bellow real loud, "TEW!" Dat mans wit' de bat on his lef ' shoulder took it off an' put it on his r'at. De catchin' man jomp up an' t'rew his mas' down an' raise a big cloud o' dust.

An' dey bot' got on each side de empire so close he could hardly breathe an' dey say in uniform: "TEW WHAT?"

He say, "Tew close to call, I ga—ron—tee you dat!"

'Fess Up

Couple year ago down in Sout' Lewisana de teacher was holdin' class, an' she ax dis li'l boy dis, an' dis li'l girl dat. An' w'en she got to Tijon she say, "Tijon, who sign dat decoration of independent?"

Tijon stood hisse'f up real careful an' look at her r'at on bot' eye an' say, "Teacher, me, I don' know, an' whass more I don' give a damn."

Dat put de teacher hot on de collar, an' she say to Tijon, "Pass you'se'f off dat seat an' brought you'se'f home, an' don' come back wit'out you' pa—pa, you year?"

"Hokay." An' SHOOM, he lef ' to brought hisse'f home.

Nex' day Tijon was back wit' his pa—pa, an' de teacher say, "Pa—pa, jus' stan' in de back o' de room an' make like you not chere." Den she ax dis li'l boy dis, dat li'l girl dat, until she got to Tijon.

She say, "Now, Tijon, like I ax you yestiddy an' I'm gonna ax you ag'in today, who sign dat decoration of independent?"

Tijon stan' hisse'f up real careful an' look her r'at on de eye an' he say, "Teacher, like I tole you yestiddy, me I don't know, an' whass more I don't give a damm."

Dat put de teachin' lady hot on de collar, an' she say, "Pa–pa, I don't like dat some a-tall. Now you took dat boy in de cloakroom an' you talk wit' him, an' you talk wit' him good."

So de pa–pa took Tijon in de cloakroom an' he say like dis, "Look here, Tijon, you know you' ma–ma don't got much educate, an' me, I got even lesser den dat. So w'en you got you'se'f in trouble you got to got out o' dat de bes' way w'at you know how. Now if you sign dat doggone paper, you go tole dat teacher!"

Question and Answer

I got a frien' wit' me w'at got a li'l boy chirren about 10 or 9 year ol'. An' you know how chirren love to lay on dey stomach an' read de funny paper on Sunday. So dis li'l boy chirren was readin' de funny paper an' he say, "Pa–pa, w'at a sweater girl, w'at dat is, hanh?"

Dat question kinda took de ol' man from behin', an' he stomble an' stutter aroun', I tole you fo' sure. Finally he say to de boy chirren, "Dass a female womans w'at work in a sweater factory. Where in de worl' did you got a question like dat?"

"Never mine where I got a question like dat," de li'l boy chirren say. "W'at I want to know is where in de worl' did you got an answer LIKE DAT?"

Physic Pickup

Dis fallow got a big furniture sto' in Sout' wes' Lewisana, an' he got furniture fo' averybody, I mean!

Avery year he go to Shy—cago to dat big convention in dat how—you—call Furniture Mart. One day he was tole—in' de boys like dis: "I pass pleas—zure, I hope to tole you! One night I got in de alley—gator in dat big hotels where I'm stayin', and dair was a female womans. OOH, MANH, you should see dat! Now I'm bashful, like all us Cajun, an' it took me 10 secon' to say, 'Honey, how come you an' me don' go got a cocktail, hanh?' "

"But she don' unnerstan' dat good English. I look her up one side, an' she look so damm good I look her down de same side. She answer me in Franch, an' I don' unnerstan' dat Franch 'cause iss Parisian Franch.

"Now me, I got determined to have a cocktail wit' dat female womans, so I got a pad wit' a pen—cil from my pock—ett an' I drew a cocktail glass. I pass it on her face, an' she cass an eye an' say, 'Ah, oui!' I say, 'Allons, less go, an' r'at now!' So we go got dat cocktail an' 11 or 10 jus' like it.

"W'en she got up to make de lady ras' room I look her up an' down dat odder side, an' iss even mo' better den de firs' side, MANH! W'en she come back I say, 'Less go got some supper,' but she don' unnerstan' nothin'.

"So I reach in ma' pock—ett an' got me dat pencil an' pad an' draw two peoples sittin' at a table wit' dishes smokin'. She say, "Ah, oui!" An' I say, 'Allons, le's go, an' r'at now!'

"After de sopper I say, 'Honey, less go dance,' but she don' unnerstan' a damm t'ing. So I reach fo' ma' pad an' draw a pitcher of two peoples dancin'. We danced 'til five or fo' o'clock, an' me, I'm a southern gentlemans, so I ascort her back to her hotel room. She pass me her key to de room, an' w'en I open de do' an' try to tole her goodnight, she reach in ma' pock—ett an' grab ma' pencil an' pad an' draw de mos' beautimous antique bed you aver laid eyes on. An' I'm still tryin' to figure out how in de worl' she knew I was in de furniture business."

Costly Cuspidor

Dey got a fallow name Isadore w'at operate a barroom saloon, an' one day his frien' name Trahan come in an' say, *"Comment ca vas,* Isidore? Manh, it dues ma' heart good to see you fix up dis place so nice."

"W'at you talk?" Isidore say. "Here it is nine o'clock in de mornin' an' you dronk a'retty. I don' fix up dis place some a-tall."

"Well, you got fo' do' now," Trahan say, an' Isidore say, "Me, I got two do' w'at I always got."

"I bet you $20 you got fo' do'."

"Put yo' money."

"Okay, dair's de fron' do' an' dair's de behin' do', hanh?"

"Das r'at. Now where dem odder two do' at, hanh?"

"You' name Isidore, dat make it t'ree do', hanh?"

"I never t'ought o' dat," Isidore say. "But sho' me dat fourt' do'."

"You see dat cuspido' on de flo'?" Trahan say. "Dat make fo' do', hanh?"

Isidore t'ought fo' a minute an' he say, "You win fair an' square. Now I'm gonna caught ma' money back from Boudreaux w'en he come in."

Soon Boudreaux brought hisse'f in fo' his mornin' pickup, an' Isidore say like dis: "Hey, Boudreaux, I'm glad fo' you to see me. How you like de way I fix up dis place, hanh?"

"W'at you talk. You don' fix up dis place some a-tall fo' 20 year."

"Well, I got me fo' do'."

"I only see two, me," Boudreaux say.

"I bet you $20 I got fo' do'."

"Put yo' money an' show me dem fo' do'."

"Okay, dair's de fron' do' an' de behin' do', hanh?"

39

"Das r'at. Now where dem odder two do'?"

Isidore say, "Whass ma' name?"

"Why, averybody know dat. Iss Isidore."

"Dat make t'ree do', hanh?"

"Okay, dass t'ree do'," Boudreaux say. "Now where dat four' do' at?"

Isidore say, "You see dat, you see dat, you see dat . . . . Doggone, dat spitoon done cos' me $40 today a'retty!"

Dock Hont

You know, lady an' gentlemans, we got a place not far from here we call False River, an' two Cajun wen' dair fo' a dock hont a few year back. Dey go over dair an' rent one dem cabin w'at dey got fo' one dollar an' a half—dem was befo' de days o' Truman an' Roosevelt, I ga—ron—tee. One dem fallow who tole de tale say, "We put ou'se'fs in bed about 7 p.m. in de evenin' 'cause we want to be sure to got up befo' dawn make a li'l bitty crack so we can got dem dock.

"An' de firs' time dawn make a li'l bitty crack we go out dair an' cass an eye on dat lake an' she's black wit' dock, I ga—ron—tee. So we go back in de cabin an' I got ma' twice-barrel Caribbean an' Jean—Baptiste got his ah—romatic shootgun an' we got out dair an' got on our belly jus' like a alligator, you know. An' we crawl on dis li'l patch o' grass an' dat li'l patch o' grass like we hide, an' we got close, close, close on dem dock, and I'm raise dat twice—barrel Caribbean an' I'm gonna got at leas' 100 on de firs' shoot becaus' dey sit so quiet out dair. An' w'en I dues dat de sky got black wit' dock—not even a poule d'eau is lef' on de lake.

"Dat put me hot, an' Jean—Baptiste he los' his temper plum'. I say, 'Don't lose you' temper,' an' he say, 'I done los' it.' I say, 'Don't you see dem cow eat dem water lily on de edge o' dat lake, hanh?' He say, 'But I ain't no cow.' I say, 'But you goin' to be one. You notice dem dock out dair ain't scared fo' dat cow, an' you goin' to be a cow.' He say, 'How I'm goin' to did dat?'

"An' I tole him, 'We're goin' to Bat—onh Rouge to de slaughterin' house how—you—call abbatoir, an' we gonna got a cowhide fo' fo' bits—fifty cents. We gonna brought ou'se'fs back here tonight an' got de same cabin, an' tomorrow mornin' we goin' to got up an' got dem dock—inside dat cowhide.'

"He say, 'Less go.'

"Dass w'at we do. We brought ou'se'fs to Bat—onh Rouge. We got a cowhide fo' 50 cents, an' we go back an' got dat same cabin fo' one dollar an' fifty cent. An' we put ou'se'fs in bed fou' t'irty in de evenin' because we want to be damm sure we got up w'en it look like dawn make a li'l bitty crack.

"An' we dues dat an' look on dat lake an' she's black, black, black wit' dock sommore, I ga—ron—tee. So we slip back in de house an' we got dat cowhide. Me, I'm in de fron' an' Jean—Baptiste de behin'. Den we took dat li'l patch o' grass an' dis li'l patch o' grass an' make like we eatin' jus' like a cow, I ga—ron—tee. An' we got close, close to dem dock, an' I'm raise dat twice—barrel Caribbean gonna got at leas' 200 dock on de firs shoot becaus' dey sit so quiet I'm gonna use bot' barrel. Jus' as I did dat Jean—Baptiste beat me on ma' back. An' I say to Jean—Baptiste, 'Raise you' gun an' shoot, manh. Do not you see all dem dock out dair on dat lake?'

"An' he say,'Fo'got about de dock. Year come de bull!'"

41

Extra Month

You know, down in Sout' Lewisana averybody like to hont, an' one day in Terrebonne Parish a Cajun brought hisse'f to de shariff.

"I'm a delegate from a whole bunch o' delegates," he say. "We want to ax you to did us a favor."

De sharrif say, "You know, I run fo' office avery fo' year, an' I'll be glad to did what I possible could. W'at dat favor is, hanh?"

An' de delegate say, "We'd like you to give us anodder mont' to shoot dock."

De shariff say, "W'at you gonna name dat mont', hanh?"

"W'at de hell you meant, shariff?"

"Look," de shariff say, "You hont 12 mont' in de year now. If you got to gat a new mont', you got to gat a new name fo' dat, hanh?"

Garbled Message

Dey got a dock hont camp near a little town in Sout' Lewisana call Florence, an' dass a high class place wit' arrow—condition, santral heat, hot an' col' runnin' . . . water, dat is, an' long distant telephone—got to be long distant, nothin' else near Florence.

De dock honters come out dair to got as many illegal dock as dey possible could did, an' dey leave one guide at de camp to answer de phone an' make sauce piquante, gumbo, stew an' cook dem rice—us Cajuns got to have rice.

An' dat remin' me about dat Cajun brought hisse'f in one dem restaurant—cafe in Lock Charles. He clam'

42

up on de stool an' a good—lookin' girl waitress lady female brought herse'f an' say, "What can I did fo' you, hanh?" An' dat damm fool say, "I want a hamburger."

She say, "All de way?" An' he say, "No, cut de rice."

Anyway, like I tol' you, dis guide got to answer dat long distant phone, an w'en it ring isse'f he say, "Hello, dair."

An' dat long distant phone say, "Dis is Houston, Taxes, callin' long distant."

De guide say, "I know dat."

Den dat long distant phone say, "You can call Mr. Smith to de phone? He dock hontin' down dair."

"Lady," de guide say, "I can't go got him. No, operation, he in de blin' an' dey took a shot at me. I ain' about to go out dair."

"Can you took a message den, hanh?"

"Oh, hell yeah. Jus' hol' you'se'f still while I go got pencil an' pepper." Pretty soon he come back an' say, "Shot de work."

"O. K. Dis is Operation—61."

"Operation 61."

"Houston, Taxes."

"Houston, Taxes."

"The calling number is Capital 2, 1234."

Dair was a dead still, an' de operation jingle de hook an' say, "Hallo, are you dair?"

He say, "Hell, yeah I'm here. But tole me, operation, how in de worl' you make a Capital 2, hanh?"

Exotic Gombo

I was rode down de road one day an' dair was a li'l boy chirren drag a bird wit' a wingspread about six

43

feets. Now I got a big cur—ous, like all us Cajun, an' I say, "Son, w'at you got dair, hanh?"

He say, "A hawk," an' I say, "A whut?"

"A schicken hawk, dass w'at I got dair."

"What in de hell you gonna do wit' dat hawk?"

"Make gombo soup."

"Oh, does hawk meat make pretty good gombo?"

" 'Bout like owl."

Shocking Intimacy

You know, de wondermous t'ing in marriage is de sacrifice de parent make to give dey chirren a educate. I got a frien' in Crowley an' durin' de depression t'ings was so bad he mortgage averyt'ing w'at he got—A-Model T Ford, crawlin' tractor, averything. Den he fine out about a school name S. M. an' U. in dat foreign country call Taxes, an' sen' his boy chirren dair. In t'ree year de boy chirren finish law school, an' he become one dem lawyer peoples an' got hisse'f a job wit' de only t'ing humble in Taxes—de Humble Oil an' Refined Company.

One day dat son ax de lagal department in dat Humble Oil an' Refined Company to go punch some hole in Acadia Parish on his pa—pa's lan', an' firs' t'ing you know dey hit de bigges' oil fiel' in Sout' Lewisana.

So de ol' man got so rich he don't know w'at to did, an' one day w'en he walk down dat main street of Crowley he meet a frien' wit' him. "You know w'at I'm gonna did?" he axed dat frien' wit' him.

An' de frien' say, "Dair ain't a bit o' tole since you got dat money w'at you gonna did."

44

Den de pa—pa say, "I gonna sen' a whole buch o' money to S. M. an' U. to show ma' 'preciate fo' de educate dey give ma' son."

An' de frien' ax, "How much you gonna sen'?"

He say, "Savan figure wit' no period in between."

De frien' say, "You don't know about S. M. an' U. Why you don't sen' it to a good school like L.U.S. here in Bat—onh Rouge?"

"Becaus' ma' son don't granulate hisse'f from L.U.S., but from S. M. an' U., dass why."

De frien' say, "Yeah, but don't you know dat at S. M. an' U. de boys an' de girls matriculate togedder?"

"I don't believe it," de pa—pa say.

"But dass not all. At S. M. an' U. de male professor can look de girl t'esis over."

An' de pa—pa say, "Iss a damm lie."

His frien' say, "You don't got to believe me. Jus' wrote you'se'f a letter to S. M. an' U. an' ax 'em. An' ax 'em if de boy an' de girl don't use de same curriculum."

"Hokay," de pa—pa say.

About a week later de pa—pa meet his frien' on de street. "I got me de answer to ma' letter in my pock—ett," he say. "Read it fo' you'se'f."

"You read it to me," de fallow say.

"I don't got to, becaus' I mesmerize avery word. Firs' dey say de boy an' girl don't got to matriculate wit' each odder any more. An' from now on only de female professor womans look de girl' t'esis over. But dey say dey can't do nothin' 'bout de boy an' de girl usin' de same curriculum."

"You see?" his frien' say. "I tole you dat. Now I suspose you gonna give you' money to L.U.S., hanh?"

"No, indeed," de pa—pa say. "I done alretty sen' it to S. M. an' U. I was young once ma'se'f."

45

Couch Confession

I got a frien' w'at live near Denham Springs w'at drive a gravel truck. He got hisse'f 11 or 10 chirren, an' since he got paid by de load he got make planty load. So he work from kin to kaint—from de time you kin see to de time you kaint.

But ma' frien' got one problem, him. He make one nightmare almos' avery night, an' each time he dream he drive hisse'f from Denham Springs to Waco, Taxes. Dass 425 mile one way—850 roun' trip. Avery night he brought hisse'f back jus' in time to wake hisse'f up an' go to work to drive dem damm gravel truck all day long 'til he wore out plum'.

So he tole his boss about de problem an' about how he don't even dare took a nap 'cause he afraid he'll go someplace.

"You better brought you'se'f to a how—you—call psychiatris'," his boss say, an' ma' frien' ax, "W'at dat is?" His boss say, "Dass one dem doc—taire gonna fine out if you got somet'ing on you' mind dair."

W'en he brought hisse'f to de psychiatris' he say, "Doc, I got me a problem." An' de doc—taire say, "Lay you'se'f down on de couch an' tole me about it while I sat ma'se'f in de rocker here."

So ma' frien' 'splain his problem to de psychiatris', an' after he bent his ear fo' 30 or 20 minute, de psychiatris' say, "You got you'se'f a problem, all right, dass fo' sho'. Now we gonna change place an' you sat in de rockin' cheer an' I gonna lay on de couch. I want YOU to ax ME if I got a problem."

So ma' frien' change place an' ax de psychiatris' if he got a problem. An' he say, "You damm right. I ga—ron—tee! Me, I got planty respec' in de community, on de directin' boa'd at de bank, a deacon at de church an' all dat stuff. Now avery night me, I got a dream where blonde, brunette, chatain, redhead female girl womans in dey negli—gee. Dey all holler, 'Let me in, Doc,' an' me, I can't afford to did dat."

An' ma' frien' say, "How de hell come you didn't call me?"

"I did," de psychiatris' say, "but avery time I dood you was goin' to Taxes."

Standby

I got a frien' w'at been hearin' 'bout dat Mardi Gras in New Or—lee—anh fo' t'ree or two year. An' one day he say, "I bleeve I gonna took ma'se'f down dair. So he come to New Or—lee—anh an' cass his eye aroun' 'til he so tired he don't know w'at to did. Pretty soon his feet begin to talk back to him, an' dass bad, you year?

So he brought hisse'f to a hotel in de Franch Quarter an' he tole de man behin' de des' he got to have a room, an' r'at now.

De man say, "You got a reserve?"

"Hell, no," ma' frien' say. "I didn't know I was gonna brought ma'se'f here 'til dis mornin'."

De des' clerk say, "Dass too bad, becaus' we take reserve t'ree or two year ahead of time. We don't even got a chair fo' you to sit on."

Den ma' frien' say, "I wanna ax you a question. Jus' suppose Praise—i—dent Reechard M. Nixonh, Praise—i— dent of de U. S. an' A. brought hisse'f here an' ax you fo' a room. W'at you gonna tole him, hanh?"

An' de room clerk say, "Well, dass different. You know I always got a room fo' de praise—i—dent of de U. S. an' A."

47

An' ma' frien' say, "Well, he ain't comin'. Gimme his room, an' r'at now!"

Trail Blazers

Years ago at a place call False River dey got two fallow wen' one day to catch deyse'f some bream perch fish. An' dey go to a Cajun name Olivier Guillaume—dass Oliver Williams in English—to rent a boat. Dey go out dair an' start to catch dem bream as fas' as dey can bait a hook, an' one dem fallow say, "Dis de bes' doggone place to fish I never saw befo' ag'in in ma' life." An' de odder one say, "Ma'se'f, I bleeve dat, too. I wish we could mark dis place so we can fine it ag'in."

"I fix dat r'at now," de odder fallow say. An' he reach in his pock—ett an' got his knife an' notch on de side o' de boat.

Soon dey got de boat so full o' bream iss about to sink isse'f, so dey pull up anchor an' head fo' home. W'en dey mos' back to de dock one dem fallow say, "You know, you planty smaht to t'ought o' dat. But jes' suppose we don' got de same boat nex' time—how in de hell we gonna fine dat place?"

Alarming Symptoms

Dis spring w'en dey got a nice sunshiney day, two lickin' pot houn' dorgs lay deyse'f in de fron' yard of a house near French Settlement relackin' demse'ves. Now I want you peoples to know a lickin' pot houn' can outrelack anyt'ing you aver saw. Dey got a cat beat all de way. An' I never will fo'got dem dorg layin' out dair in dat fron' yard drinkin' in dat sunshine an' relacking demse'ves.

On de fron' porch o' de house dair was a whole bunch o' teenage chirren wit' a record player goin' full blas'. You could hear it 10 mile nort' an' sout', eas' an' wes' an' up an' down. All o' de chirren would do de watusi, twinkie, jerky, swim, twis'—nobody dancin' wit' anybody else. Look like dey all runnin' got a drink o' water, or somet'ing.

One dem ol' lickin' pot houn' raise his head up—jus' a li'l bit cause he don' want to lose his relack—flop his head back down an' say to de odder, "You know, if we did dat dey'd worm us, I ga—ron—tee!"

Good Hontin'

Many year ago w'en de auromobile was known hardly any a-tall some in Lewisana, dis fallow got two li'l boy chirren, one 'laven an' one tan. An' dey don' want but one t'ing in dey life, an' dass a tan-gauge shootgun to help de pa—pa shot dem goose.

Well, de pa—pa make a pretty good season o' trappin' dem muskrat, an' he decide he got enuf to buy one tan—gauge shootgun fo' bot' chirren. "But," he say, "you mus' not fight over dat shootgun, you year?" An' de boys say, "Oh, no, we will not fight some once a-tall any. We'll took turns, I ga—ron—tee."

So he haul off an' go got him a tan—gauge shootgun,

36-hinch barrel, hammer look like a ear, iss so big.

De li'l boys iss so proud o' de shootgun, but dey don' got no shell. So dey steal some egg from dey ma—ma, go sell dem egg an' buy some shell. Iss too late to shoot dem gooses, so dey decide dey gonna shoot dem lapin, which is rabbit in Lewisana. So dey took deyse'ves to a place where de hill stop an' de marsh begin isse'f 'cause dey know dey got planty rabbit dair.

An' here come one dem firs' Model T come along, somet'ing dey never saw befo' ag'in in dey life. Iss runnin' lickety—split down dem road—fas' like hell—20 mile an hour. It ain' nuttin' but a dirt road, an' dat Model T raise a cloud o' dus' you can see fo' tan or nine mile, I ga—ron—tee.

An' de li'l boy ax his older brot'er, he say, "W'at dat is, brot'er, hanh?" De brot'er say, "Me, I don' know, but w'en he pass I gonna let him have it, I ga—ron—tee. You go hide behin' dat big pine tree over dair." So de li'l brot'er go hide, an' de man come by in de Model T Ford an' de boy lower dat ten—gauge shootgun an' BLOOM.

Well, de manh ran off de road an' turn over on one dem li'l hill an' jomp out an' run jus' as fas' as he can. An' de li'l boy come from behin' de tree an' say, "Did you kill it, brot'er?" An' he say, "I don' know, but I made it turn dat man loose, I ga—ron—tee!"

Chow Hounds

Not long ago over at Cape Kennedy dey hired a whole bunch o' dem Cajun to go to work on dem rocket over dair. Dey work dem 'bout t'ree week, an' SHOOM, dey run 'em all off an one time, because avery time dey holler LAUNCH dey go got somet'in' to eat.

Backfire

Years ago I lived in Crowley, Lewisana, an' I know a fallow w'at had a poultry shop down dair befo' dey had superin' market an' t'ings like dat. An' you went an' bought you' stuff live if you want to, an' dey had some few hen an' dock an' gooses an' turkey dress, an' sometime he got by wit' quail an' t'ing like dat.

Well, he had avery kine of poultry, an' one day he'd do good, some day he would not do too good a-tall, none, any. An' one Sadday he had de bes' day he never had befo' ag'in since he open dat poultry shop. An' he was jus' about to close, because all he had lef' was one ol' hen.

An' a li'l ol' lady hit dat do' BLIP an' say, "You not close, hanh?" An' he say, "No, brought yo'se'f in." She say, "You got a hen?" An' he got dat one ol' hen lef'. He say, "Of cou'se I got a hen!" "Well, I hope iss big enuf. I got company comin'. I would like fo you to weigh dat hen."

So he reach down in dat ice, got dat ol' hen, put it on de scale an' he say, "Fo' an' t'ree-quarter poun'." An' she say, "Well, I don't t'ought dat's big enuf. I got some company, like I tol' you."

He say, "You want one bigger den dat?"

"Please."

So he put dat hen back in de ice an' SHOO, SHOO, SHOO, SHOO, SHOO summore, put de same ol' hen back on de scale an' put his t'umb wit' it, you know. An' he look at dat scale real careful-eyed an' he say, "Six an' t'ree-quarter poun'."

Well, she look at him, den she look at de hen, den she look back at him summore, up at de ceilin', back at de flo', averywhere. An' she say, "Give me bot' dem damm ol' hen."

51

No Contest

You know, in de Silver War Lewisana haul off an' succeed from de Union real fas' w'en dat gun go off at Fort Sumpter, an' dem Cajun join up r'at now, 'cause dey wanted to see w'at dis was all about.

My gran'pa join up an' wasn't in de war two week befo' dey capture him an' send him way up Nort'—in Mitchigan—to a prisoner—of—war camp. He got up dair an' dey sent him out on a work detail an' he gave 'em hell. He say, "You know, us Rebels nelly ran you Yankees into de Atlantic Ocean at Chickamauga. We jus' beat de hell out o' you at Chickamauga, I ga—ron—tee. If we'd jus' kep' on goin', if we had any lines o' supply, we'd a whupped you r'at den an' dair fo' good 'til it was pitimous. We jus' beat de hell out o' you Yankees at Chickamauga."

Well, dey jus' got to took him off de work detail . . . he had t'ings so upset dat dey couldn't work, de guard couldn't do anyt'ing but hol' de gun on dem. Dey wait a couple o' week an' put him out dair ag'in. But he wasn't out dair t'irty minute befo' "Us Rebels beat de hell out o' you Yankees at Chickamauga, I ga—ron—tee!" An' he jus' gave dem all de devil he can t'ought about, an' dey got to bring him back in.

An' finally after about six mont' o' dat de commandin' officer sent fo' him an' say, "Look, we got to got you to stop irritatin' all dose peoples like dat. We can't got anyt'ing done because of your 'Us Rebels beat de hell out of you Yankees . . . .' Now dair's no way fo' you to got back dair, so we would like fo' you to join de Union Army an' we'll give you $5,000. We would like fo' you to stay here an' be one of de guard."

He say, "Hell no. Us Rebels gave you Yankees hell at Chickamauga."

Well, dey sen' him back out dair an' he commence doin' de same t'ing, disruptin' de whole prisoner−o−war camp. An' de C.O. sen' fo' him sommore an' he say, "Look, we'll give you $10,000 an' make you a sergeant if you'll join de Union Army so we'll got you to shot up about de Rebels givin' us Yankees hell at Chickamauga."

He say, "Make me a sergeant? I always wanted to be a sergeant. O. K., dass a deal." An' de C.O. say, "Well, all right, de deal is dat you don't talk about you Rebels givin' us Yankees hell at Chickamauga." An' my gran'pa say, "Dass r'at. I won't did dat."

So dey make him a sergeant an' he go out on de work detail fo' de firs' time and ack real good. But he wasn't out dair t'irty minute befo' he say, "You know, dem Rebel beat de hell out o' us Yankee at Chickamauga, I ga−ron−tee!"

High Stakes

Savarel year ago in Sout' Lewisana dair was a high school football distric' in which was a high school football team dat was suspose to win all iss game dat season. But it did not dit dat—it los' some. An' I want to tole you, it had a real fine football team—big, fas', smaht, an' de fastes' quarterin' back in de state o' Lewisana on dis football team dat was suspose to win all iss game.

We got anodder team in dat distric' dat wasn't suspose to win some game a-tall, any, none. It was suspose to lose all iss game, but it didn't did dat. It win some, an' dey got to have a playoff to decide who de champeen o' de distric' was. An' I want to tole you

53

peoples somet'ing. You t'ink dey take football serial up Nort'—in Shreveport? WHOO! Dey don't know de meanin' of de word. Dose Cajun took dat football real serial down dair. Dey bet dey horse, dey wife an' dey chirren on a ordinary season game. But dey bet dey house, wife an' chirren, milkin' cow, crawlin' tractor, T-Model A Ford, schicken an' dorg on a playoff like dis.

Now de team dat was suspose to win was los' 6-0 on a playoff game, an' dair was lesser den two minute to play. An' de team dat was suspose to los' was win 6−0. An' I wanna tole you, dat coach w'at coach dat team w'at was suspose to los', he was happy, yeah. But narvous—WHOO! Walk up an' down de sideline an' say to hisse'f, "Manh, I hope dat slow quarterin' back (de slowes' man on de team was his quarterin' back) keep de ball on de groun' even w'en he can't stood it sommore. He got de game win."

So he sent one dem runnin' gard in dair an' he say, "Go in dair an' tole dat slow quarterin' back to keep de ball on de groun' an' don't chunk no fo'wa'd pass."

He say, "Hokay."

So he wen' in dair an' he say, "De coach say don't chunk no fo'wa'd pass. Keep dat ball on de groun'. He don't want dat team dat was suspose to win but lose got dat ball."

An' de slow quarterin' back of de team what was suspose to lose but win say, "Hokay."

He doin' jus' fine an' he keep dat ball on de groun', but he saw his bes' frien' girl up dair in de grandstood watchin' him, an' he on de 18-yard line an' he say, "I got nothin' to lose, me. Jus' one mo' fo'wa'd pass."

So dat slow quarterin' back o' de team what was suspose to lose but win he jus' r'ar back an' CHOO chunk a fo'wa'd pass r'at into de arm of dat quarterin' back w'at was de fastes' man in de state of Lewisana on dat team

54

w'at was suspose to win but los'. So he start out down de sideline lickety split, but befo' he reach dat 50-yard line dat ol' slow quarterin' back done catch him an' BLAM. Den de whistle blow an' de game over.

We all go to de dressin' room because de player got to change clothe. An' de coach of de team w'at was suspose to win but los' come in dair an' he say to de coach of de team w'at was suspose to lose but win:

"Ma' frien', I would like to ax you somet'in'. Would you please let me know how it is dat dat ole slow quarterin' back you got—so slow he can't catch a cold—overtake ma' quarterin' back, de fastes' man in de state of Lewisana, run de 100 in 9.7. He catch him befo' he reach de 50-yard line. Will you please tole me how he did dat, hanh?"

Well, de coach w'at coach de team w'at was suspose to lose but win, he tole de coach of de team w'at was suspose to win but lose: "Ma' frien', iss jus' like dis. W'en you' boy caught dat ball he was runnin' fo' a touchdown. But ma' ol' slow quarterin' back, he was runnin' fo' his life, I ga—ron—tee!"

Johnny-on-the-Spot

Dis happen on de Labor Day weeken', w'en de state police had to work 12 hour on an' 12 off. An' I got a frien' on Friday night got to work all night. At 8 o'clock in de mornin' he come in off de Interstate an' brought hisse'f into one dem combination rest—runt, cocktail loonge, barroom—saloon cafe. He order some coffee, but a frien' wit' him say, "Don't drink no coffee. Have a beer wit' me."

"But I'm in uniform," he say.

"Well, go take it off," de frien' say.

So he say, "Hokay," an' took off his uniform. After a few hour he say, "Look, iss 10 o'clock. I got to brought ma'se'f home to res' befo' I got back tonight. I got me a bran' new petroleum car, a bran' new radar, a bran' new rad—io, an' a bran' new syringe, an' I'm gonna catch me some dem devil tonight, I ga—ron—tee."

An' he say to his frien', "Don't got on dem highway if you drink too much, you year?" An' de frien' say, "Don't worry none a-tall any. I ain't gonna did dat."

Well, dat state policeman got hisse'f some sleep, an' dat night he got in dat bran' new petroleum car an' went out on de Interstate. He got a nice straight stretch an' he park on de shoulder. He fix his radar jus' r'at, an' he look out de behin' view mirror. An' here come a car WHOO, it was really tearin' up, you year? He look on his radar—97 mile per hour—an' he say, "Manh, I'm gonna got him!"

He notice de light gettin' real bright in his car, you know, an' he look on his behin' view mirror an' dat car was on de shoulder wit' him! An' he talk wit' hisse'f, he say, "Dat car's on de shoulder wit' me! Dat car gonna hit me! An' ZHOOM, he roll down on de flo' of his car underneat' de dashin' board, an' BLOOM, dat fallow hit him an' knock him 300 feets, an' he could hear dat odder car turnin' over FLIPPETY FLOPPETY, FLIPPETY FLOPPETY, an' he crawl out o' dair bruise, but not hurt bad, but he look over at dat odder car an' he know dey mus' all be dead after it was turn over eight or seven time. De car was layin' on iss side, an' jus' as he got dair de door open an' out crawl his frien' w'at he had dem beer wit' dat mornin'.

De frien' took one look at him an' he say, "How in de worl' did you got here so quick? Dis wreck jus' happen!"

Poor Prospect

Not long ago I had a young frien' w'at finish de L.U.S. Law School, you know, an' got to be one dem lawyer peoples. Now he spen' all his money goin' to school, an' w'en he got t'rough he had nothin' lef ' but a lot o' faith in hisse'f. But he don't got nobody come to his office, an' he about to lose his discourage plum'. One day he look out de window an' a fallow is comin' down de walk dair to his office. An' he say, "Looka dair, a client!" So he reach dair an' got de foam w'at was lyin' on his des', an' w'en de fallow come in he say, "Sit you'se'f down." Den he turn to de foam an' he say, "No, no, hell no, I ain't gonna cut my fee from $50,000. No, not $49,500. Hokay, brought you'se'f by an' gimme a li'l check fo' maybe $10,000 or $15,000 to seal de deal."

Den he hang up an' say to de fallow, "Now, my frien', w'at can I did fo' you?"

An' de fallow say, "I'm from de foam company. I wanna connec' you' foam up."

Limited Jurisdiction

I got a frien' dat live in a li'l town in Sout' Lewisana, an' I want you all to know dat he's not an alcoholic, no. He's not a drunkard, too—he's a winehead. He drink dat ole cheap wine, de cheaper de mo' better becaus' he can got mo' of it, you know.

An' befo' he took his firs' drink in de mornin' you can smell him at leas' t'irty t'ree feets away—terrible—dat ole sour wine, you know. One Sadday mornin' he wake hisse'f up an' he felt bad WHOO-EE. An' he talk wit' hisse'f while dem picture is rattlin' on de wall from his pulse—beat. "I feel bad," he say to hisse'f. "I'm gonna go to confessin'."

So he reach onder de bed an' got half a fif' dat ol' Sweet Lucy an' CHOOM, he drink it down. His courage begin to come back all de way, an' he got up an' shaved an' showered an' put on his blue serge suit. Den' he foun' anodder fif' Sweet Lucy he had hid from hisse'f. He drink it down 'til his courage was back, an' good. Den he went to de church (I ain't no Cat—lic, but I been dair!) Dat confessional got one li'l room where de confessor go. Iss got anodder room where de confessee, or de pries', sits. In between dey got a six—by—four wire mesh—cover window dat you can hear t'rough, but not see t'rough.

De father got to got up close, close, close, because I wanna tole you, dem confessin' peoples don't talk loud, no. Ma' frien' in dair say, "Father, WHOO-EE." Dat mus' knock dat pries' out, you year, an' he lean over de odder side, his side, an' he say, "Yes, my son."

Ma' frien' say, "I done haul off an' sin bad, WHOO-EE," an' Father lean over one side an' say, "Son, have you killed anybody?"

"Oh, no, Father, I ain't kill nobody, WHOO-EE," an' Father say, "Hokay, son, dass enough confessin' fo' de week."

So ma' frien back out dair an' walk out de church. He meet one his frien' on de way in and he say, "You goin' to confessin', hanh?"

He say, "Hell, yeah!"

Den ma' frien' say, "You kill anybody?"

He say, "Hell no, I ain't kill nobody."

Ma' frien' say, "Well, dair ain't no use in goin' in dair. All he's hearin' today is murder cases."

Emerald Èquine

Years ago befo' World War Twice I lived in Crowley, Lewisana. Now aroun' Church Point an' Carencro an' Rayne an' Crowley you'd see so many black buggy wit' beautimous buggy horses as you would auromobiles—maybe more. An' Sunday when you pass by de Cat'lic Church at Church Point at 11 a.m. Mass an' dey got 100 buggy an' t'ree or two auromobiles.

Now I got a frien' w'at live down dair at Baptist Academy, between Bunkie an' Church Point, an' how dat place got dair I don't know. An' when he went to Mass one Sunday a frien' wit' him say, "Why you don't brought you'se'f to de big fais do-do tonight at Lawtell, hanh?" An' ma' frien' say he gonna did dat, becaus' he proud of his wondermous chestnut—colored horse which he curry an' comb all de time an' make her shine an' glisten.

Ma' frien' got dair early an' find a nice comfort place to leave his buggy an' unhitch his horse an' make her comfort.

Lemme tol' you somet'ing, a fais do-do iss a country dance where averybody go—mama, papa, grampa, all de chirren—averybody.

Ma' frien' went into dat dance an' he pass pleas—zure, I ga—ron—tee. He did not miss one dance. About eight o'clock he run out of steam, an' he went out to de buggy where he had some steam out dair—in a gallon jug. He took a look to see how his mare was doin', an' somebody done haul off an' painted her a bright green all over. It mos' kill him dead, so he say, "I can't stood dat." He almos' had a apologetic stroking r'at dair.

SHOOM! He tore back on dat dance flo' an' he hollered, "Who painted ma' mare green?"

59

But dey couldn't hear him wit' dat SHABOOM, SHABOOM, SHABOOM. So he got on de bandstood an' committed de cardinal sin. He stop de music. A verybody turn aroun' an' look at him an' he yell real loud, "I want to know who painted ma' mare green?"

An' a great big fallow—'bout six foots eight inch, weigh 320 poun'—walk up dair an' say, "I painted you' mare green. W'at about dat?"

An' he say, "I jus' wanted to let you know she's dry an' ready fo' de secon' coat."

Useless Credentials

You know, I never will fo'got, I got a frien' w'at got a great big rice farm—about 1,500 acre o' rice. Also, too, he raise dem Santa Gertrude certified cattle. He proud o'dat farm, an' anybody w'at come dair he glad to show 'em w'at he got.

One day one dem bureaucrat w'at work wit' de federal D.A. department o' adgi—culture knock on de do'. Ma' frien', lookin' at de idiot box to caught de noonday news, hear a FLAP, FLAP, FLAP, FLAP, FLAP on de do', an' he open it an' say to de bureaucrat dair, "W'at can I did fo' you?"

An' dis bureaucrat got one dem laminated card, ZOOM, chunk it r'at in ma' frien' face an' say, "You saw dis card?"

An' ma' frien' say, "Of cou'se I saw it. Iss r'at in ma' eye."

An' de bureaucrat say, "Dis card give me de r'at to look at anyt'ing I want to on dis farm. It give me de aut'ority to look all over de place, an' you can't did nothin' about it."

Ma' frien' say, "Go ahead an' look 'til you' eyeball fall out on de groun'. Iss all right wit' me."

Well, de bureaucrat lef' an' ma' frien' got back to see de news. Den he year de bureaucrat holler, "He'p me. Please he'p me." Jus' like John McKeithen w'en he run fo' governor. Ma' frien' go out dair an' dis bureaucrat done got hisse'f inside de corral where dey got five bull. One dem bull was chase t'ree step behin' him tryin' to make it two. An' de bureaucrat holler as he steam pas' ma' frien', "He'p me. Please he'p me. Won't you he'p me?"

Ma' frien' watch him go by one time an' he don't said nothin'. But de t'ird time he holler to de bureaucrat, "Show him you' card. Show him you' damm card!"

Never T'aught o' Dat

Dis Cajun live down dat swamp near Maurepas, an' fish an' hont an' trap all his life an' he never got to town much. But he cut his own wood. He was fishin' wit' a fallow he was guidin' down dair, an' dat fallow tole him, "Say, w'at you ought to got is a chain saw."

He say, "A chain saw? One dass got a chain on it?"

He say, "Yeah."

An' dat Cajun say, "I gonna got one o' dat nex' time I brought ma'se'f to town."

Well, he brought hisse'f into Denham Springs one day, an' he pass at de hardware sto', an' in dat hardware store dair was a soldsman dair, an' he axed him, he say, "You got a chain saw?"

An' dat soldsman say, "I ga—ron—tee! Dat chain saw we got will cut six cord a day at leas', an' probable mo' den dat."

61

He say, "You mean to tole me it'll cut six cord a day?" An' de soldsman say, "I ga—ron—tee! Cut at leas' dat an' more if you're good." An' de country Cajun say, "I'm good!"

So he bought de chain saw, an' he worked de firs' day wit' dat chain saw, an' all he cut was two cord of wood. "Well," he say, "I can't stood dis." Nex' day he got up befo' daylight an' he got out dair an' it look like dawn make a li'l bitty crack. An' he work wit' dat chain saw plum' slap 'til dark—an' he got mos' fo' cord o' wood.

He say, "Look at dat! I'll got it tomorrow." Nex' day he got up befo' it was ever t'ought about gettin' daylight, an' he went to work wit' a lantern an' he cut wood 'til de lantern burn plum' out all dat night. W'en he check his wood nex' day he got no mo' den five cord.

So he say, "I'm gonna took dat chain saw back—dat fallow ga—ron—tee it'll cut six cord o' wood." So he brought it back de nex' day to dat hardware sto' in Denham Springs, an' he fine dat same sellin' man w'at's in dair an' he say, "You tole me it would cut six cord an' it don't did dat. I got me five cord, but it was a big day w'en I did dat, an' you ga—ron—tee dat chain saw."

An' de sellin fallow say, "I wonder w'at can be de trouble wit' dat saw." An' he grab dat ripcord—dat startin' cord—an' pull it an' it go "b—r—r—r—r—r."

An' dat Cajun say, "W'at in de worl' is dat noise?"

Holdout

You know, lady an' gentlemans, it happen not far from Bat—onh Rouge, in de distric' court in one dem parish we got down dair. Dis happen on a trial. Dair was a lawyer down dair, an' he was a stomp down good lawyer, him. He loved criminal law, an' he would make a good criminal hisse'f. He loved to take a case an' win it—an' mos' of de time he did win it. He never los' anybody to de hot squat, an' he'd take dem cases an' go to court an' w'en he got paid off he'd come get wit' all us boys, an' we'd go to de barroom saloon cocktail loonge an' he'd tole us about averyt'ing an' we'd have a good time—pass pleas–zure. He was one de boys all de time.

One day dey had a case comin' to trial dat averybody in de whole town, de state an' de nation knew he was guilty. He had committed a terrible crime, and no lawyer would even look at him, let alone touch de case—an' you know he mus' have been guilty.

So dey had to appoint a lawyer, an' dey appointed dis frien' wit' me an' he say, "No, I can't took dat. Ain't no way to win. I t'ink he's guilty ma'se'f, an' I can't convince ma'se'f dat he's not. Dass de way I win ma' cases—w'en I convince ma'se'f ma' client is not guilty—but dis fallow is guilty, I mean."

An' de judge say, "You contemp' of court if you don't, an' dat ain't all. You not gonna try sommore cases 'roun' here."

Well, he had to took de case. He say, "W'at I'm gonna did to got dat mans off wit' somet'ing to keep him off de hot squat?" It was a murder case—horrible. He say, "Let me t'ink." An' he did. He t'ought an' t'ought an' t'ought. An' he say, "I got it! Lemme got dat jury lis' I got to fine somebody in dat jury—dass w'at iss all about. An' I got to fine a man dair. You know, iss got to be unamous—12—for 'em to convic' him of murder, but only nine fo' manslaughter. I'm gonna try to got him off wit' manslaughter. Dass w'at I'm gonna did." He look at dat lis' an' say, "Ho! Dair he is. I've done a lot fo' him, I ga–ron–tee. Lemme go see him tonight." An' late dat night he go to see dat Cajun on de jury lis'. He knock on de do' an' de man say, "Brought you'se'f in," an' w'en he did he say, "I'm glad fo' you to see me, I ga—ron—tee." An' dat Cajun say, "I'm glad fo' you to see me too." An' de lawyer say, "I got to ax you to did somet'ing." He say, "Go ahead. You know I got to did it. You got me off o' too much trouble a'retty. I'll be glad to did w'atever you said."

De lawyer say, "Hokay. You gonna serve on de jury." He say, "W'at trial? An' how you know dat?" He say, "Dass all right how I know dat." An' he tole him w'at trial an' dat Cajun say, "Oh, no, dat man's guilty."

He say, "Shot up, don't even sugges' dat to you'se'f. You gonna serve on dis jury." An SHOO, SHOO, SHOO, he peel off some money an' pay him. "Dass half of it," de fallow say. "Oh," de juryman say, "dat make it different r'at dair." An' he say, "Tole me mo' about dis case."

De lawyer say, "You got to hole out for manslaughter—manslaughter." He say, "W'at dat is, hanh?" "You don't got to know w'at dat is. Jus' remember, MANSLAUGHTER."

Well, dey choose de jury an' it didn't took long. An' t'ings looked bad, WHOO! I mean. Dat poor defendant sat dair look like he gonna go to de hot squat, an' dis on top o' dat. It look bad fo' him even w'en ma' frien' took his handkerchief an' crush an onion real good an' cry like a baby w'en he hol' dat onion up to his nose to address de jury. He talk about averyt'ing excep' dat mans on trial—but he cry about averyt'ing—an' de jury cry wit' him.

An' de judge w'en he charge de jury tole 'em averyt'ing excep', "If you don't brought in a verdict o' guilty wit' capital punishment I gonna hol' you in contemp' o' court."

So de jury lef'—dat was in de mornin'—an de jury at 5 p.m. sen' word back dey couldn't reach a decide. An' de judge say, "Lock 'em up sommore." But on de fif' day dey sen' word dey had reach a decide.

De judge say, "Brought 'em in." So dey brought deyse'f in, an' de judge say, "Gentlemens, have you reach a verdict?"

An' de foreman stood hisse'f up an' say, "I ga—ron—tee!"

De judge say, "W'at you' verdict is, hanh?" An' de foreman say, "We, de gentlemans of de jury, fine de defendant guilty o' manslaughter."

Well, de courtroom wen' wild. De judge had an apologetic strokin', an' de defendant fainted r'at dair. Averybody excep' his lawyer, he was jus' cool an' collec'. He had pack up averyt'ing in his briefcase—one piece o' paper—all ready to took out o' dair.

An' late, late, late t'ree or two night later, ma' frien' go to dis Cajun house w'at was on de jury, an' dey glad to see each odder sommore. He say, SHOOM, SHOOM, SHOOM, SHOOM, an' give him de odder half o' de money. He say, "You don't know how proud I am of you, I ga—ron—tee. Iss wonderful you hol' out fo' manslaughter. I don't know how you did it. I jus' want to congranulate you one more time. I know it was a hard job."

Dat Cajun say, "You jus' don't know HOW hard. You know, 11 o' dem wanted to turn dat man loose."

Greased Lightning

You know, I got a frien' w'at fine hisse'f in Atlantic, Jaja, an' how he aver got to dat place I don't know. But he want to brought hisse'f back to New Or—lee—anh, an' he go up to dat hairline des' at de

65

arrowport an' he say to de fallow stoodin' dair, "Ma' frien', you got some plane to New Or−lee−anh, hanh?"

"But fo' sho'."

"W'at time de nex' plane took off?"

"Nine twenty-five."

"An' w'at time id arrive in New Or−lee−anh?"

"Nine twenty-six."

"T'ank you vary much," ma' frien' say as he wheel hisse'f an' leave dat des'. Dat man didn't tole him about de different of one hour in de time.

He wait 'til anodder man is on de des', an' he go back an' ask, "You can tole me w'at time de nex' plane leave for New Or−lee−anh?"

"Nine twenty-five."

"An' got to New Or−lee−anh?"

"Nine twenty-six." So he wheel hisse'f aroun' ag'in an' he took hisse'f outta dair.

He wait 'til dey busy wit' a lot o' peoples workin' dair, an' he say to a t'ird man, "Ma frien', w'at time de next plane leave for New Or−lee−anh?"

"Nine twenty-five."

"An' reach New Or−lee−anh?"

"Nine twenty-six. I can sol' you a ticket to go dair?"

But he shook his head and wheel to took hisse'f outta dair. "No, t'ank you vary much," he say. I just want to go out dair an' see dat son−of−a−gun take off, I ga−ron−tee!"

Brash Lothario

I got a frien' w'at is a roughin'neck, he works in de oil fiel'. One day he was in town an' he pass a barberin' shop an' dair was a female womans manicuris', OHH MANH! A good-lookin' t'ing, I ga−ron−tee. So he wen' in dair, brought hisse'f to de chair an' he say to de barberin' man, "Shot de work." "You want a manicure?" de barberin' man say, an' ma' frien' say, "Of cou'se. I tole you to shot de work."

So she brought herse'f over dair an' he look her up one side, OOH BOY! Now he bashful, like all us Cajun, an' it took him 14 or 12 secon' to make up his mind. "Honey," ma frien' say real sociable—like to dat good—lookin' female womans manicuris', "How come you an' me don't go got a sirloin steak, hanh?"

She say, "I can't did dat."

"How come?"

" 'Cause I make marriage an' ma' husban' would not like dat, no."

"Oh," he say, "You don't got to tole him w'at you did. Jus' tol' dat fool somet'ing, anyt'ing." He say, "Honey, I know a place de moon shine in de marsh t'rough dem cypress tree on de Golf of Mexico 'flectorizin' on dat water. Less you an' me go dair an' court up a storm, hanh?"

"I can't did dat," dat good—lookin' female womans manicuris' say, w'ile all de time dat barberin' man work on him.

"Honey," he say, "like I'm tole you befo', you don't got to tole dat fool nothin' 'bout where you go an' w'at you done did. Tole him anyt'ing, he'll believe you."

She say, "How come you don't tole him you'se'f? He's shavin' you r'at now."

Proof of Pudding

Once upon a time a fallow was sit on de bayou bank one day wit' a fishin' pole fishin'. It been rainin' nine or eight day, an' dat bayou swell good wit' dat water, you know. An' anodder fallow rode up on his horsebackin' ride an' he say to de fallow fishin', "Ma' frien', you know a shallow place where I can cross dis horse to got over on de odder side, hanh? I got some cattle over dair I would like to cass my eye on."

An' dis fallow fishin' hisse'f say, "R'at by dat stump over dair is shallow, shallow, shallow."

So de fallow on horsebackin' go over dair an' jomp his horse in de bayou an' KABLOOM! de horse, man an' all, got out o'sight, jus' his hat lef' on de water, an' w'en he brought hisse'f up he say wit' sputterin', "I'm gonna unclam' dis bayou an' beat de devil out o' you, I ga—ron—tee."

"How come?" de fishin' man say.

"Becaus' you tole a doggone lie, dass how come."

"I did not lie," de fishin' man say, an' dat fallow on horsebackin' say, "You mean to tole me you did not see me an' dat horse go plum' out o' sight? An' jus' becaus' of dat secon' lie I'm gonna did it ag'in."

"I did not tole a lie," dat fishin' man say. "Jus' a li'l while ago I saw a duck wit' leg fo' or t'ree inch long wade all de way across."

Relapse

In World War Twice we had a shortage of doctor—vary bad. Dey took a lot o' dem into de sarvice, an' we had a real shortage, you year? Peoples couldn't enjoy poor healt' so much, dey had to work. An' de medical school did not shorten de cou'se in medicine—don' misunderstan' me. Dey granulated 'em from de school of medicine, but dey shortened de internship, you know, w'en dey start workin' on live peoples.

An' I never will fo'got, down dair where I live in Livingston Parish, dey didn't hardly have any doctor a-tall—jus' one. An' dey had to have anodder doctor, an' dey sent a young mans dair to work one side o' de parish, an' de odder doctor work de odder side.

Now, iss a big parish, an' he had two mont' intern at Charity Horse—pistol in New Or—lee—anh, an' he got dair an' he was scared, but he had granulated from medical school, an' he was ready. So he pass out dem aspirin—befo' we had virus. One day he was sittin' in dair an' a Marine—one dem big fine Cajun boy rotated back from Guadalcanal or one dem island down in de Souse Pacific an' he had somet'ing bad wrong wit' him he t'ought—Chinese crud or somet'ing.

An' he came dair to see de doc an' he SHOOM t'row open his shirt an' he got a bad rash on his ches'—dass w'at he got—look like de 14—year itch. An' he say, "Doc, will you please look at dis an' tole me whass wrong wit' me? Please doc, will you did dat?"

De doc got dair an' he look real close. He got his magnification glass an' he look t'rough dat an' he look up at dat fine young mans an' he say, "Ma' frien', have you had dis befo', hanh?"

An' de young man say, "Hell, yes, I've had it befo'."

"Well," de doc say, "you got it ag'in, I ga—ron—tee."

Anyt'ing for a Gag

Cajun will do anyt'ing wit' dey wonnerful sense o' humor jus' fo' you to ask 'em "How come?" An' den SHOOM! Dey lower de boom on you. Dis happen jus' wes' of Denham Springs, Lewisana. Denham Springs is legally dry—legally, I said, an' East Bat—onh Rouge is legally wet. Some year ago dey got a li'l cocktail loonge an' dey had a li'l barmaid in it cute like hell—smaht alec, flip an' fly, had a answer fo' averyt'ing—it didn't make any different. She even furnish you a question if you didn't have dat.

Dair was one Cajun dat come in dair avery day to got a bottle of pop wit' foam on top an' a single shoot o' whiskey—chase it wit' de pop. An' she gave him so much hell, even I felt sorry fo' him. An' he never said a dammed word—he jus' looked at her.

An' one day he came dair an' dragged a 20—foot log chain wit' a clickety, clickety, clank, clank, blop! an' sat hisse'f down. An' she talk wit' herse'f, she say, "I KNOW he wants me to ax him how come he drugged dat log chain in dair, but I ain't gonna did it."

She say, "W'at you want?"

He say, "Gimme a bottle o' pop wit' foam on top." He drink dat, pick up de log chain, clickety, click, clank, clank, an' drag it back outside.

She say, "I didn't ax him, ha, ha, ha, ha, I did not ax him." An avery day fo' 10 day he return clickety, click, clank, clank, an' she talk wit' herse'f sommore. "I ain't gonna ax him." She gave him hell, but she didn't ax him about dat log.

Avery day he drink dat beer, den drag dat log chain back out, clickety, clickety, clank, clank. An' on de 'laventh day here he come, clickety, clickety, clank, clank. An' she cannot stood it sommore, an' he say, "Gimme . . . "

She say, "Shut yo' mout'. How come you drag dat log chain in here, hanh?"

He say "I'd look like hell tryin' to push it in here, I ga—ron—tee!"

Kill the Goose

You know, down in Plaquemines Parish I was down dair in Buras—not too damm much lan' an' a heluva lot o' water, dat's fo' sho', an' I guess de wides' place on one side is about a mile. Dey had two farmer dair live nex' do' to each odder wit' small farm 'bout 40 acre apiece.

An' one o' dem got a horse—not much of a horse, part quarter horse, part horse. An' his neighbor come 'roun' dair one day an' say, "You know, dat li'l ole pony look good. Would you sol' him?"

"Hell, yeah, I'd sol' him."

"How much you want fo' him?"

"Two hunnert an' fifty dollar."

"I'll give you two hunnert."

"You got you'se'f a horse."

Well, de neighbor wen' an got his trailin' truck an' took de horse over to his farm. 'Bout t'ree or two week later de fallow w'at sol' de horse was havin' a drink wit' his neighbor an' he say, "Dat horse look mo' better den it did w'en I sol' it to you. Would you sell it back to me, hanh?"

"Hell yeah."

"How much you want fo' him?"

"T'ree hunnert an' fifty dollar."

"I'll give you t'ree hunnert."

"You got you'se'f a horse."

So he took de horse back home an' he had him 'bout a mont' an' de neighbor come over dair an' say, "Manh, I wan' to tole you, w'at you been doin' to dem horse? He lookin' mo' better avery day. Would you sol' him?"

"Well of cou'se I'd sol' him."

"How much you want fo' him?"

71

"Fo' hunnert an' fifty dollar."

"I'll give you fo' hunnert."

He say, "You got you'se'f a horse." So he picked him up an' he brought him back home, an' he kep' him fo' about a mont' or t'ree week.

An' de fallow w'at had de horse original took hisse'f over dair an' he was jus' finish curryin' an' shinin' him up real good an' manicurin' his toenail an' averyt'ing. He say, "Manh, dat horse look good yeah. I jus' got to bought him back. Would you sol' him to me?"

"Of cou'se I'll sol' him to you."

"How much you want?"

"Five hunnert an' fifty dollar."

"I'll give you 500."

"You got you'se'f a horse."

Well, he wen' back to his house an' he jus' barely got him unloaded w'en here come dis fallow from Taxes go t'rough buyin' horse avery now an' den—wit' a great big trailer. He say, "Dass a nice-lookin' horse you got dair. How much you want fo' him?"

Now de farmer didn't want to sol' him, but he say, "I'll jus' go ahead anyhow. I'll ax him somet'ing ridiculous." So he say, "Twenty five hunnert dollars."

He say, "I'll took it. Help me load him in de trailer."

After he got him loaded, de fallow from Taxes brough hisse'f down de road an' stop at de neighbor house. He say, "You got any . . . ?"

De fallow saw dat horse in de trailer an' he didn't answer him, he jus' say, "Where'd you got dat horse, hanh?"

He say, "From you' neighbor."

He didn't even tole him goodbye, but jomp in his country Cadillac—dass a pickin' up truck—an' he rolled up to his neighbor house. He jomp out, leave iss motor

72

runnin' an' averyt'ing, an' he say hot on de collar, "W'at do you mean solding dat horse like dat? Do you realize dat bot' of us were makin' a damm good livin' out of him, hanh?"

Last Straw

I got a frien' name Aubrey Laplace dat got a store in St. Gabriel Lewisana, r'at sout' o' Bat—onh Rouge. You don't see many o' dese sto' any mo'—really ol' country sto' dat got 22—feet ceilin' an' dey got shelf all de way to de top. An' dey still got dem ladder w'at you rode up an' down on an' got stuff off de top shelf. Iss a old—fashion country sto' an' a wunnerful country sto'.

You know Aubrey, he got to where he was havin' a li'l trouble on figurin' de profit on his candy, becaus' he had a lot of candy, an' he had a lot of chirren comin' in gettin' dem candy. But he didn't show some profit—none, a-tall, any. So he decided dat w'at he had better did is put dat on de top shelf—27 feets high—an' Aubrey a very met'odical man, very met'odical. He got a ladder he keep on de odder side o' de store. So he put de candy up dair where de chirren all know where it is. But he got to go got it—dey can't got it by deyse'fs, you know.

An' one day he was stood in dair—got dat ladder way down de odder side o' de sto' where it suspose to be. He was stoodin' dair an' a li'l boy about 10-year-ol' came in an' Aubrey say, "W'at you want, son?"

An' he say, "I want a dime wort' of licorice."

"O. K." An' SWOOM! He go down an' got de ladder way down dair, he carry de ladder back to de odder side where de candy is, clam' de ladder, reach in dair an' got dat can where he's got dat licorice stored up in, come back down, come to de counter dair, count out 10 stick

73

black licorice, wrap dem in paper sack. Den he say, "Gimme a dime, son." De li'l chirren give him a dime, he say, "T'ank you," an' rang it up on de cash re−gister. He pick up dat can, go back up dem ladder, put dat licorice up dair where it belong an' SHOOM, come back down de ladder an' take dat ladder back where it belong on de odder side o' de store, you know.

Den he turn hisse'f aroun' to talk wit' me, an' in come anodder li'l boy 'bout nine−or eight−year−ol'. He say, "Wa't you want, son?"

"I want a dime wort' o' licorice." SHOOM, he go got dat ladder from de odder side o' de store, brought hisse'f back, put dat ladder where dat candy is on de shelf on dis side de sto', clam' up dair, got dat can o' licorice, brought hisse'f back down an' comes to de counter an' count out 10 stick o' licorice, put it in a paper sack bag, say "Ten cents." De li'l boy give him a dime an' SHOOM, he rang it up in de cash re−gister. He pick up de can o' licorice, clam' back up dat ladder, put it up dair where it belong, clam' down, pick dat ladder up an' put it where it belong on de odder side o' de sto'!

He turn aroun' an' say, "Juice−tanh . . . " an' here come anodder li'l boy 'bout 10−year−ol' an' behin' him a li'l boy 'bout six. He say, "Son, w'at would you like hanh?"

"I want a dime wort' o' licorice."

He say, "Hokay," an' he about to lose his patience, plum'. He go got de ladder, brought it back aroun' dair, clam' up dair w'en he got dair, pull dat can o' licorice out, brought hisse'f back down, put 10 dem stick in a paper sack an' say, "Ten cents, please." An' de li'l boy gave him a dime. SHOOM, he rang it up in de cash re−gister. Den he tole dat li'l boy 'bout six, "I reckon you want a dime wort' o' licorice, hanh?"

An' de li'l boy say, "No."

74

He pick up de licorice, go got dem ladder, put de licorice up, brought hisse'f back down de ladder, pick de ladder up, brought it all de way across de sto' where it belong.

Den he come back an' say, "W'at would you like to have, son?"

An' he say, "I want a nickel wort' o' licorice."

Identical Twins

Dair was a Cajun down in Sout' Lewisana not long ago, an' he had twin horse—dass rare—an' he always was talkin' about, "You know, I jus' can't tole dose horse apart, you know dat?"

Well, anodder Cajun wen' to see him an' say, "I'm gonna he'p you. Less measure dem horse."

"I done did dat."

"Less do it ag'in. You don't know nothin'. I'm gonna he'p you r'at now."

He say, "Ho—kay." An' bot' of dem are 15½ han's high on de dot.

He say, "We can't tole 'em from dat. Bot' de same high."

He say, "Whut you better did is cut one o' dem tail—trim de tail."

"Hell, I did dat, an' de damn t'ing grow r'at back avery time."

"Well," he say, "trim a mane dair."

"I did dat too, an' de damn t'ing kapt growin' back."

"Did you measure how long dey are, hanh?"

"No, I never t'ought about dat. Less measure 'em r'at now." Well, dey measure 'em, an' one is jus' 'zactly

75

t'ree fourt' of a han' longer den de odder.

He say, "You see dair? Dass easy. Now you can tole dem twin apart from now on."

An' de owner say, "You know, I always did t'ought dat black horse is longer den dat white one, you know dat?"

Overexposure

Down where I live dey got dat daylight savin' time, an' I wanna tole you, it play hell. A fallow tole me, "Look, I don't know whut I'm gonna did."

I say, "What's de trouble?"

He say, "De daylight savin' time is ruinin' de farmin' peoples, you know." Dis fallow farm all de time an' make his livin' dat way.

I say, "Whut you talkin' about?"

He say, "One more hour of sunshine jus' about to burn everyt'in' I got up."

Speed Limit

Long time ago down near Rayne an' Church Point, Lewisana, you saw mo' o' dose blacktop buggy den you could auromobile—a lot more. A frien' wit' me had one dem blacktop buggy. He live between Church Point an' Rayne, an' one day he brought hisse'f into Rayne wit' his whole fambly. Dair was his wife, a li'l be—be in her lap, an' two chirren sittin' in de back wit' dey feets hangin' over de back, you know. An' he drove in dair wit' dat ole horse CLICKETY, CLICK, CLICK, CLICK—not at a dead trot, jus' a shufflin' walk.

76

An' he saw de firs' speed limit sign he never saw befo' ag'in in his life w'en he drove into Rayne. Dair was de speed limit sign say 35 MILE PER HOUR. He say WHOO–E–E–E an' he stop dat ole horse to a dead still, I ga–ron–tee, an' he turn to his wife an' say, "Ma–ma, hol' dat li'l be–be close wit' you." Den he open dat li'l curtain an' he lean t'rough dair an' he tap bot' his chirren on de head an' he say, "Bot' han's. I want you to hol' on. No messin' aroun', you year?"

Den he turn aroun' an' she say, "W'at you gonna did, hanh?"

An' he say, "T'irty five mile an hour. I'm gonna see if I can make it, you year?"

Persistent Movie-Goer

Not long ago in Bat–onh Rouge I got a frien' w'at go to de movie pitcher show all de time. But dair was one show w'at brought isse'f dair an' I notice he go to see dat show avery day—but he didn't stay fo' de whole show. But avery time dat show start he's back in dair sommore, an' I begin to wonder w'at de hell goin' on dair.

So about de fourt' day I see him dues dat I ax him w'en he brought hisse'f out, "Dass a pretty good show, hanh?"

He say, "It ain't so damn good."

"Well, how come you go to avery one dem show?"

He say, "Well, dey got a scene in dair where de railroad track run in fron' of a house, an' dair's a female girl womans in dair an' WHOO, you talk about a pretty t'ing. An' she start to took her clothe off, an' jus' w'en she got to where she goin' took 'em all off, here come de

77

train WHOO WHOO, r'at in fron' of me. An' I figure if I kept goin' long enuf dat damn train is gonna be late, I ga—ron—tee!"

Reasonable Deduction

You know, not long ago dair was a young fallow who was an apprentice carpenter—wen' up to a construction job an' applied fo' a job wit' de carpenter foreman. He say, "I would like to got a job as a apprentice carpenter."

De foreman say, "You qualify?"

"Hell, yeah. I would not be here if I didn't qualify. I got my paper."

He say, "Hokay," an' he han' him one dem li'l carpenter apron an' a hammer an' he say, "Go over dair an' help 'em wit' dat siding on de house w'at dey buil' dair."

He fo'got all about de apprentice, den he look over dair an' dair dat Cajun is. He put a nail in dair an' den he go KA—BLOOM, KA—BLOOM, KA—BLOOM, KA—BLOOM, KA—BLOOM. He put anodder one in dair an' he chunk it over his shoulder into de grasses. An' he watch him an' he do dat avery odder nail practical—into de grasses over his shoulder. An' dat foreman walk over an' he say, "W'at in de worl' do you dues, hanh? Put dem nail up dair, you nail one avery now an' den. Den you put some up dair, you chunk 'em over you' shoulder into de grasses. How come you do dat?"

An' dat Cajun say, "I put dem up dair, an' if it face r'at I nail it in. If it face toward me, iss not fo' dis side o' de house an' I jus' chunk it away."

An' dat foreman say, "Look here, fool, why you don't save dem fo' de odder side o' de house, hanh?"

Paratrooper Dilemma

In World War Twice I was in de harmy six mont', 11 days, four hour an' 20 minute. A lot of us Cajun went in dair an' one o' 'em got in dair who don't like de harmy some a-tall.

So dey ax fo' volunteers fo' de paratroopers, an' he don't know w'at a volunteer is an' w'at a paratrooper is. Dey say, "Hol' up you' han' fo' a volunteer." SHOOM, up his han' go an' he's in de paratrooper.

Well, he foun' out after he got in dair w'at a paratrooper is susposed to did—he suspose to jomp. Well, one day dey ran him over de ob−stackle cou'se up an' down dem rope, an' he tole de top sergeant who was his drillin' master, "Man," he say, "w'en I'm gonna jomp, hanh? I been practice not one time a day, but 100 time, I ga−ron−tee!"

An' I want to tole you, dat sergeant got mad like hell fo' dat, you know, an' he tole him, "You jomp from a tower firs'," an' dat Cajun say, "I jomp from dat wit'out dat umbrella, w'at you talk about?"

So one day de sergeant brought 'em all together an' say, I wanna tole you somet'ing. Dis is you' granulation day. You went out las' night on spacial pass. You drink dat pop wit' foam on top, I know you feel good today. You gonna make you' firs' jomp. An' dat firs' jomp is on you. After dat de res' is on us—de U. S. an' A. paratrooper harmy.

"Now we want you to know we gonna make dis t'ing as safe as we possible could. You got a chute on you' back. Reach back dair an' felt dat . . . You felt dat?"

An averybody say, "Y−a−a−a−a."

An' he say, "You notice in de fron' here dey got a rippin' cord? An' w'at you dues w'en you jomp from dis

79

plane you reach dair an' you got dat rippin' cord an' you count ten real slow . . . one, two, t'ree, fo', five, six, seven, eight, nine, ten an' CHOO'. Pull dat rippin' cord. Dat chute gonna open up, an' you float in dair to de eart' in dis clear fiel' we got where dey ain't a pebble stone in dair big as a 50—cent piece so you won't broke somet'ing.

"Pick you' chute up an' walk in any direction, don't make some different. De truck park all 'roun' dat big fiel'. You got on dem truck an' dey gonna brought you r'at back to camp. ANY QUESTION?"

Dat Cajun say, "Hell, yeah! How come we got anodder chute on our belly stomach up here, hanh?"

An' de sergeant say, "I'm glad you ax dat. Dey ain't a remote possible dat de chute on you' back ain't gonna open isse'f up. So in case it don't open isse'f up you got the immer—gency chute r'at dair in fron', an' you got a rippin' cord on dat. Now if dis one don't open isse'f—but iss gonna open isse'f—don't worry about dat, you reach down an' grab dat rippin' cord an' you count slow just like I tole you to ten—SLOW. Den SHOOM, pull dat an' you fine dat chute gonna open isse'f up r'at in you' face, float you down in de fiel'. Walk in any direction, don't make some different 'cause any way you walk we got truck all de way aroun' dat fiel' gonna brought you r'at back to camp. ANY MO' QUESTION?"

No mo' question. W'en dey get dat Cajun on dat plane dey got to help him off a little bit, you know, an' he jomp an' he follow instruc' r'at down to de letter an' de number. He grab dat rippin' cord an' he count slow jus' like de sergeant tole him: "One, two, SHOOM, ten." He pull dat rippin' cord, an' ain't somet'in' happen some a-tall. So he reach an' get dat odder one r'at in front of him on his belly stomach, an' he count slow ag'in, "One, two, SHOOM, ten," an' den he pull dat rippin' cord. But somet'in' don't happen ag'in too.

80

An' he say, "Wat you t'ought about dat? Dat lyin' son—of—a—gun sergeant. I bet dair ain't truck number one down dair to took us back to camp either."

Sure—Fire Remedy

I got a frien' dat not long ago start to have some terrible nightmare. He dream avery night dat somebody was under his bed. Now I don't know why he dream somet'ing like dat, but avery night han'—runnin' he dream somebody was under his bed.

So he go to a psychiatris' an' say, "Look, I undertan' you charge pretty good. I got a problem an' a bad one. How much do you charge?"

"Well," he say, "about $100 a visit."

Ma' frien' say, "How many visit it gonna took?"

He say, "I don't know. Tole me you' problem."

"Well," he say, "ma' problem is dis. Avery night w'en I go to bed an' put ma'se'f to sleep, I dream somebody is under ma' bed. WHOO, I can't stood dat. So I wake up an' firs' look under dair an' nobody dair. Got back in bed, sleep sommore, dream ag'in somebody under ma' bed. I jus' don't got much sleep."

De psychiatris' say, "Dass bad."

Ma' frien' say, "Well, how long it gonna took to did somet'ing?"

"Oh," de psychiatris' say, "maybe 20 or 19 visit."

All de time ma' frien' cackalate dat come to $2,000, an' he don't t'ought he can stood dat, so he say, "I see you later," an' brought hisse'f outta dair fas'.

'Bout t'ree week later dat psychiatris' go down de street an' meet dat Cajun an' he say, "Were you not in ma' office, hanh, not long ago?"

An' he say, "Dass r'at." "You were in dair about a problem. You had a nightmare? You dream avery night you put you'se'f to sleep an' you dream sommore somebody under you' bed. An' you got up an' look an' ain't nobody dair. You jus' los' all you' sleep. How come you didn't brought you'se'f back? Did you got rid o' you' nightmare?"

He say, "No, but I got it cured."

"Oh," de head-shrinkin' man say, "you wen' to anodder psychiatris'?"

Ma' frien' say, "No, a frien' o' mine cured me, an' it cos' me jus' exactly one dollar an' fifty cent."

An' he say, "Well, would you mine tol' me?" He want to fine out some kine of new treatment. Dem psychiatris', dey got to keep up wit' averybody.

He say, "No, I don't mine tol' you. Cos' me t'irty minute work on his part. He got him a saw an' come an' saw de legs off ma' bed. Now dair ain't a chance of somebody bein' under ma' bed, I ga—ron—tee!"

Phantom Monster

I can't help but t'ought about dat frien' wit' me dat live in Opelousas, Lewisana, an' he go to Detroit, Mitchigan, an' how he foun' dat place I don't know. An' he got a job up dair wit' de auromobile transport peoples, you know. Dat is dose big trailin' truck w'at brought all dose bran' new auromobile down Sout'. An' he got de job wit' de onderstood dat avery two week he gonna got to go to Opelousas on his way to Beaumont an' Houston, Taxes, an' he can see his wife an' chirren w'at he got dair.

Well, dey fo'got to consider dey got to unlearn him how to drive Cajun style, dat take two week. Den dey got to taught him how to drive Yankee style, an' dat take two mo' week. An' de firs' trip he got from Detroit is to Miami, Florida, not to Beaumont an' Houston, no. An' he wore out fo' road map tryin' to figure how to go t'rough Opelousas, but he don't made it.

So w'en he brought hisse'f back iss been six week since he been home, an' he mad—he mad like hell, I ga−ron−tee. An' he walk up to dat man an' say, "How come you tole me dat damn lie, hanh?"

De man say, "Which one?"

He say, "You know which one. You tole me avery two week I'm gonna got to go t'rough Opelousas on ma' way to Beaumont an' Houston to take all dem bran' new Cataract auromobile. It been six week since I been home, an' dem chirren liable to ax dey ma−ma who dat man, an' she may not know, an' dass bad."

"I'm so sorry about dat," de man say. "An' I'm so sorry you didn't brought you'se'f back mo' early becaus' I got a trip dat's gonna lef' in two hour, an' I know you too tired to took dat out."

He say, "Who say I'm tired? Me, I'm in good shape, I ga−ron−tee!" Well, de man feel real sympathize to him an' he say, "Hokay, go got you'se'f 'about 40 wink an' brought you'se'f back an' you can took dem bran' new Cataract r'at to Beaumont, Taxes."

Well, he take 20 wink 'cause he don't want to miss a damn t'ing, you know. An' he got back dair an' he got on dat trailin' truck an' he say, "Opelousas, here I come, WHOO BOY! Ol' lady, I know you gonna be glad to see me, yeah!"

An' he do jus' fine 'til he got about 40 mile from Opelousas at 10 p.m. in de nighttime, an' de headlight on dat trailin' truck go FLICKETY, FLICKETY, FLICKETY, FLICK, an' dey go plum' out. An' he pull on de side an' come to a dead still an' walk across de road an' look at

83

dat truckload o' bran' new auromobiles an' he talk wit' hisse'f, he say, "Look at dat! Dis Cajun snakebit by a whole basketful o' snake, I ga—ron—tee. I can't stood dis." An' he notice dat dat top auromobile is face de same way wit' him, you know. He say, "Lemee see . . ." an' he run back across de road an' he turn dat headlight on an' he can see fo' a mile—an'—a—half down de road. He say, "Oh, manh! Wonder how come dat safety man didn't t'ought of dat?" An' he got back in dat trailin' truck an' he say, "Opelousas, here I come. WHOO BOY!"

He not gone vary far befo' he notiss a car brought isse'f up de road, an' it got about a half mile from him an' leave de road, bugety, bugety, bugety . . . cross de cow pasture, you know. An' he pull his truck to a dead still an' reach down fo' de immer—gency broke so it won't roll, an' he run across de road an' across de cow pasture an' holler at de manh, "You hurt, ma' frien'?"

De fallow say, "No."

He say, "W'at de matter, you got a blowin' out?"

De fallow say, "Nothin' blowin'."

"You' steerin' wheel broke?"

"Nothin' steerin'."

He say, "W'at in de worl' happen den?"

De fallow say, "Well, iss like dis. Me, I was brought ma'se'f up de road, an' you, you was brought you'se'f down, an' me, I figured if you was half as wide as you is tall, I better give you planty o' room, I ga—ron—tee!"

Anatomy Problem

Not far from Bat—onh Rouge we got a town how—you—call New Roads, an' I got a frien' w'at live dair, an' one day I brought ma'se'f dair to see him. W'en

I got dair I see him walkin' down de main street, an' he got a New Or—lee—anh Tamms—Picayune daily paper under his r'at arm. An' I can tole de way he look he look fo' dat smaht Cajun w'at avery town got one of—if it's a Cajun town. If it ain't, it's a smaht somet'ing else.

An' I decide I'm not gonna leave him see me—I'm gonna eavesdrip an' see w'at goes on. Well, he finally find dat smaht Cajun an' say, "I'm glad fo' you to see me, I ga—ron—tee."

An' dat smaht Cajun say, "I'm glad fo' you to see me too. W'at you wanna know, hanh?"

He say, "How you know I wanna know somet'ing?"

An' dat smaht Cajun say, "Look, you would not look fo' me unless you want to know somet'ing. Go ahead an' ax me, I'm boun' to know."

Ma' frien' say, "Hokay, can you tole me where a female woman's 'yet' is locate, hanh?"

"W'at you say?"

"I ax you a silver question, an' I want a silver answer. Can you tole me where a female woman's yet, y—e—t, is, hanh?"

An' dis smaht Cajun say, "Female woman, dey don't got some yet."

Ma' frien' say, "Look, jus' because you don't know where iss locate dat don't mean she don't got one, I ga—ron—tee." An' a big argue start.

Dat smaht Cajun say, "Oh, no she ain't."

An' ma' frien' say, "Oh, yes she has."

"Oh, yeah."

"Oh, no."

"Yeah."

"No."

"Hell, yeah."

"Hell no."

Well, dat smaht Cajun realize he not gonna got someplace like dat, an' he say, "Look, you so smaht askin' me dem fool question, how you know a female woman got a yet?"

Ma' frien' say, "I didn't t'ought you'd aver ax me." He reach under his arm an' he grab dat daily New Or−lee−anh Tamms−Picayune, open it up on de fron' page an' he say, "Cass you' eye r'at dair an' rub you' eyeball on dat fron' page. It say dat a female woman been shot wit' a .38 special, an' de bullet is in her YET."

Misleading Ritual

Dey got two li'l boy w'at live nex' do' wit' each odder, an' dey play all de time. Dey never got some argue 'bout somet'ing a−tall. Dey never got fis'fight in de eye. Dey love each odder. Dey play all de time. Dass on Monday, Tuesday, Wednesday, T'ursday, Friday an' Sad'day. But on Sunday, WHOO, hell broke loose, becaus' one o'dem is Cat'lic an' one is Met'odis', an' dey got to make a separate to brought deyse'f to church. So dey raise so much sand it begin to look like gravel, an' dass bad, you know.

An' dey ma−mas is worried 'cause dey gonna give deyse'f a fever. Now one day pa−pa, he smaht, you know—schoolteacher—he say, "How come you don't sen' 'em to one church on Sunday, an' den bot' to de odder church nex' Sunday?"

An' de ma−mas say, "I never t'ought about dat."

So de firs' Sunday dey brought deyse'f to de Cat−lic church, an' dat li'l Cat−lic boy, OHH, was so proud to have his frien' wit' him, I ga−ron−tee! An' dey walk in dat church, fine a place where dey gonna sit demse'ves down—how—you—call a pew. An' dat li'l Cat—lic boy genuflect, you know, dass w'en you make like you kneel, but you don't quite make it.

An' dat li'l Met'odis' boy never see dat befo' ag'in in his life, an' he say, "W'at dat is, hanh?"

Dat li'l Cat'lic boy axplain it to him so careful, becaus' he want his li'l Met'odis' frien' to enjoy dem Mass an' brought hisse'f back w'en iss his turn. Den dey sat deyse'ves down—don't got de seat warm up good an' averybody stan' up.

De li'l Met'odis' boy never see dat befo' in his life, an' he say, "W'at dat mean, hanh?"

An' dat li'l Cat'lic boy axplain dat so careful an' so sweet de way he dues dat. An' all t'rough Mass dat li'l Met'odis' boy want to know w'at dis mean, an' w'at dat mean, an' dat li'l Cat'lic boy, oh, was he sweet de way he axplain averyt'ing.

De nex' Sunday dey brought deyse'ves to de Met'odis' church an' dey walk in an' dair's a printed program an' dat li'l Cat'lic boy never saw dat befo' ag'in in his life. He say, "W'at dat mean, hanh?"

An' dat li'l Met'odis' boy so sweet he axplain dat to his li'l frien' becaus' he wanted to be sure dat li'l Cat'lic boy brought hisse'f back wit' him nex' Sunday w'en iss his turn.

Den averybody stan' up an' sing a song. De li'l Cat'lic boy never see dat befo' an' he say, "W'at dat mean?"

An' dat li'l Met'odis' boy so good de way he axplain dat. An' averybody sit deyse'ves down, an' de choir stood isse'f up in front of averybody an' sing a song.

Dat li'l Cat'lic boy never saw dat befo' ag'in too, an' he say, "W'at dat mean?" An' de li'l Met'odis' boy axplain dat real careful.

De choir sit isse'f down an' de preacher walk across how you call de cockpit, an' he reach in his pock—ett an' grab a great big watch an' put it in fron' of him like dat. An' dat li'l Cat'lic boy say, "W'at dat mean, hanh?"

An' dat li'l Met'odis' boy say, "Not a damn t'ing!"

Well-Mannered Rookie

You know, de Cajun is de frien'lies' peoples in de worl' an' de U. S. an' A. too. Dey got a Cajun rookie in de army an' one day he pass hisse'f by a big shoot general wit'out salute. Dat put de big shoot general hot yeah, an' he pull dat rookie up short. "How long you been in de army, soldier?" he say.

"T'ree week."

De big shoot general t'ought for a minute an' he say, "Whass you name, private."

Dat rookie smile an' hol' out his han' to de big shoot general. "Broussard, an' you?" he say.

Sizing Him Up

I got a frien' w'at brought hisse'f to Church Point, an' he cass an eye on a man stoodin' by de corner and he ax him like dis, "Ma' frien', you can tole me where Francois Prudhomme live, hanh?"

He say, "Francois Prudhomme? Lessee. Yeah. You go fo' 'bout a mile dair an' you gonna see a oak tree, an' on de lef' is dat li'l yellow house where he live."

Ma' frien' say, "T'ank you vary much," an' de man say, "Wait. Francois Prudhomme, you say?"

88

Ma' frien' say, "Dass r'at."

An' de man say, "Dat instruc' I give you don't right. Francois live on de islan' part, him. You got to brought you'se'f aroun' de behin' side an' you goin' see a li'l yallow house wit' a chinaball tree. Dass where he live."

Ma' frien' say, "T'ank you so much."

"Wait a minute," de fallow say, "you specify Francois Prudhomme?"

"Dass r'at."

"Well," de man say, "dass me. Whut you want?"

Unfinished Sentence

I got a frien' wit' me in Loff—i—yette w'at got a wife took herse'f down to New Or—lee—anh to look at some dem markland house in de Gordon distric'. Dey rich like hell—strike oil, you know—an' dat womans want to buy how—you—call a showin' place.

Well, dis real astute broker got hol' of her an' show her a beautimous home dair. He took her t'rough dat, an' w'en dey move out de bedroom he say, "Now dis is de playroom an' den."

She cass bot' eye on him r'at now an' she make spoke to dat real astute agent, "An' den WHUT?"

Alley Gator Miracle

Down in Rayne dey got a fallow brought hisse'f to New Or—lee—anh fo' de firs' time. He pass in one dem apartment sto' an' he stop an' stare at dem alley gator. Pretty soon one dem alley gator stop isse'f, an' a ol' lady

89

all bent over wit' a cane pass herse'f inside dat t'ing. Den a light fash, de do' close an' she disappear.

While de fallow ju' stood dair an' cass an eye on dat alley gator do', dat do' open an' doggone, out come a young womans saxy like averyt'ing. "How you like dat," dat fallow say to hisse'f as he walk away. "Me, I shoulda brought ma' ole lady to put in de alley gator, I ga—ron—tee."

Same Principle

You know, dey got a school in Sout' Lewisana where de teachin' lady ax a li'l boy name Placide, "Whut did Davy Crockett kill hisse'f, hanh?"

An' Placide say like dis, "He kilt hisse'f a Cajun."

"Dat don't r'at," de teacher say. "He kilt hisse'f a bear."

An' Placide say real hot on de collar, "Well, if Hebert don't be a Cajun, w'at he are?"

Family History

I got a frien' name Melancon, pronounce Mu—lanh—sonh, w'at don't got much educate, him. An' one day he brought hisse'f to his hometown liberry an' ax dat liberry lady like dis, "Brought me a copy of *Das Kapital* by Karl Marx."

Dat liberry lady almos' los' her spoke, plum', she so sopprise dat a fallow like Melancon w'at don't got much educate ax fo' dat complicate book. So she say to

90

Melancon, "Are you sure you want *Das Kapital*? Dass some pow—ful readin', yeah."

"Brought me de book an' don't gimme some argue," Melancon tole dat womans. "Dey said it was all about my wife relatives name Bourgeois."

Wrong Refugees

Avery time dair is how—you—call a cats—sass—trophy dis story pop up about de man perch hisse'f in de tree wit' de water lappin' at his foots after a hurricane or flood hit aroun' dair. An' some rescuer row up in a boat an' dey holler to dat fallow perch in de tree, "Are you a refugee from Crowley?"

An' de fallow say, "No, I'm a Aucoin from Mermentau."

King's English Franch

You know, dey got a fallow from Rayne study up on his high falutin' Franch—w'at you call de king English Franch—an brought hisse'f to New Or—lee—anh to dem fancy Antoine Restaurant. W'en he eat hisse'f dat good meal wit' Oyster Rockinfallow an' glass port wine how-you-call Spinach o' 1927 he ax de waitin' faller fo' de check like dis: "*Donnez moi l'addition, s'il vous plait.*"

An' dat waitin' man lean over an' whisper in his listen like dis: "You brought you'se'f out dat door dair an' took a right at how—you—call dat corri—door an' den took de firs' do' to you' lef' an' dass it, r'at dair."

Ear-Poppin' Antidote

Dis Cajun name Ro—bair w'at brought hisse'f to de arrowport in Loff—i—yette gone pass to de Wes' Coast, him. He make trans—fer at New Or—lee—anh, an' w'en dat arrowplane fly low over de Rookie mountin' de sewardess pass out some schewin' gum. "Dis gonna keep you' ears from poppin' at high attitudes," axplain dat womans.

W'en de plane hit de runaway Ro—bair unfas' his sat belt an' brought hisse'f to de sewardess. Den he make spoke like dis "Miss Sewardess, please, you can tole me how I gonna got dat schewin' gum out my ear, HANH?"

Right in His Eyes

Out in de bayou country of Sout'wes' Lewisana, a preacher met one dem sammy pro bessball player on de street, an' he spoke wit' him like dis: "Telesmar Boudreaux, how come you play dat sammy pro bessball on Sunday instead o' brought you'se'f to church, hanh?"

An' dat bessball player axplain, "Well, you see, Father, iss like dis. Sunday is our bigges' day, it. Dass de only holly day w'en we can got de peoples out an' took de mos' gate receipt, us. After all, Sunday is you' bigges' day too, HANH?"

Dat preachin' fellow scratch his head, den he say, "But dair's a different, Telesmar. I'm in de right fiel' on Sundays."

Telesmar raise his eyebrow, he so sopprise, an' he tole dat preachin' man, "Me an' you both. An' ain't de sun hell out dair?"

Drawing the Line

Dey got a fallow w'at pass hisse'f by dat insane as—lum in Pineville, an' w'en he got r'at outside de groun' one dem rear tire go s—s—s—s—s, an' he put on his immer—gency broke an' brought his car to a dead still. So he got out dair an' saw he done hauled off an' got a flat tire, an' after a few hells an' damns he got off his ches' he got his jack an' lug wrench out de rear compart an' go to work change dat flat tire.

Well, he put dem lug up on de fender, an' w'en he reach for dem he knock 'em off an' dey roll PLUNK, PLUNK, PLUNK, PLUNK in dat ditch by de highway full wit' water.

So wit' a few mo' hells an' damns he commence feelin' aroun' in de water fo' dem lug w'en all of a quick he notiss a fallow stoodin' behin' de fance in dat insane as—lum lookin' at him.

"Hey, ma' frien'," dat man behin' de fance say, "why you don't take one lug off each o' dem odder tire an' use dem on de tire you jus' change, den w'en you pass at a fullin' station you can got some mo' lug."

So dat fallow w'at los' de lug was relieve like anyt'ing to got dat good advice, an' he say to de fallow stoodin' dere on de behin' side o' de fance, "Ma' frien', dass a wondermous idea. Tole me, you not a inmate o' dis institution, hanh?"

"Eat fo' sho'," de fallow behin' de fance say. "I may be crazy, but I ain' stupid, no."

Astute Storekeeper

One dem counterfeitin' Texan got hisse'f on a savan—day dronk, an' befo' he soberin' hisse'f up he whip up a batch of $12 bills. So averybody in de counterfeitin' ring t'ought about how dey gonna got rid dem $12 bill, an' one dem fallow say, "Less take us a run over to Sout' Lewisana an' fob 'em off on dem Cajun down dair." So dey brought deyse'fs to de bayou country an' pass at a crossroad grocery operate by Placide Arceneaux.

"Could you give me change for a $12 bill?" one dem fallow say very sly.

Arceneaux scratch his head an' say, "But fo' sho'. How you want dat, t're fo', fo' t'ree or two six?"

Powerhouse

Not long ago one dem nuclear—power ship visit New Or—lee—anh, an' a Cajun from Church Point put his whole fambly in de auromobile an' come down to took a look at de nuclear ship tie isse'f up at Poydras Street. W'en he got to New Or—lee—anh he brought hisse'f to a dead still by a policeman cop an' he say, "Ma' frien', you can tole me where is dat nutria power ship? Me, I got to see how dem li'l animule can run a big boat all by deyse'f."

Science Vindicated

You know, lady an' gentlemans, down in Sout' Lewisana we got a lot o' different kind o' Cajun peoples—doc—teur, shoemaker, teacher, lawyer, scientis', an' I got a Cajun frien' what is sharp, WHOO! He's a scientis' by hisse'f. He spear—a—ment all de time. He been lookin' at space fo' de las' t'irty t'ree year, an' he see a lot of it too, you year? He spear—a—ment wit' all kine o' t'ings. Not too long ago he got a bran' new spear—a—ment, an' he cannot did it in Sout' Lewisana 'cause his spear—a—ment call fo' a great big roun' rock stone an' a hill w'at he can roll it down.

Well, he ain't got no rock stone in Sout' Lewisana; he ain't got some hill, too. So he come up Nort', way up North'—aroun' Shreveport—an' he gonna conduc' his spear—a—ment. He got up aroun' Shongaloo, an' he foun' a hill w'at got a great big rock stone on dat—jus' w'at he want. An' r'at at de bottom o' dis hill dey got not a town but a li'l community aroun' dair. Dair's a fullin' station, a barberin' shop, a blacksmit' an' a church house.

So he got a pry bar, you know, an' he go up dair an' he pry dat stone 'til he got it loose, an' SHOOM, it go down de hill. It run r'at t'rough at de blacksmit' shop firs', an' dey got a horseshoe on de tong, hit his anvil, turn de blacksmit' aroun' kinda crazy like—he catch dat horseshoe in his han', look at it fas'er den you aver saw anybody in you' life, an' turn it go. It wen' on t'rough de barberin' shop an' dat man got a roun'—de—worl' haircut r'at dair.

Go t'rough de fullin' station, an' r'at behin' dat Cajun is BUGETY BOO, BUGETY BOO, BUGETY BOO run r'at behin' dat stone t'rough de blacksmit', de barberin' shop, de fullin' station, an' dat stone ran r'at into dat church where dey havin' a P. T. an' A. meetin', an' dat stone run ZHOOM r'at down de aisle an' brought isse'f to a dead still against de fireplace. An' dat Cajun was r'at behin' Averybody got up an' crowd aroun' an' he say, "Stan' you'se'f back! I'm conductin' a scientific spear—a—ment an' got to look r'at now."

Averybody stood deyse'f back—dey don't know whuss goin' on. An' he take his han' an' rub it all aroun' dem stone, dat way, dis way, all aroun', an' he didn't miss one inch o' de stone.

So he stood hisse'f up, look at averybody an' he say, "Dass r'at. No moss!"

Lost, Strayed or Stolen

You know, lady an' gentlemans, I got a frien' an' he got a li'l boy chirren an' one day las' year he brought hisse'f home from school an' he say, "Pa—pa, I got a problem."

Pa—pa say, "Well, we all got problem, son."

"But you jus' don't unnerstan', pa—pa. I got 12 problem."

Pa—pa say, "W'at you meant by dat?"

He say, "Rit—ma—tick. I got 12 problem r'at chere. De teacher done tole me dat she want to fine de common denominator avery one dem 12 problem."

His pa—pa say, "WHOO! You all still lookin' fo' dat damn t'ing? We was lookin' fo' dat w'en I was a boy."

Journalism Peoples

One upon a time dair was a li'l boy chirren name Tijon, an' Tijon got one ambish in his life. He want to be one dem journalism peoples. He want to wrote somet'ing. An' one day w'en he brought hisse'f to school dair was a school teachin' lady female womans dair say, "All right, chirrens, we're gonna all wrote how you call a t'eme or a t'esis of a hessay or a story. An' w'at we gonna did, we gonna put a whole bunch o' li'l pieces o' paper in

96

hat cheer, an' you gonna reach you'se'f in dat hat wit' yo' han' an' you gonna pull one li'l piece o' paper out o' dat, an' dass w'at you gonna wrote you' t'esis or t'eme."

Well, manh, Tijon could not wait to got his han' in dat hat. In fack, he want to put bot' han' in dair WHOO BOY! Come by dair SHOOM, reach in dair, got one li'l piece paper. He busy like a bee open dat t'ing up an' he fol' it out an' his face fall so hard BLIP, you can hear it, becaus' he got a word an' he don't know w'at de hell dat word mean. 'Cause he got to wrote a story on dat, an' de word w'at he got is "frugal," F–R–U–G–A–HELL.

So he brought hisse'f home an' he walk in de house an' his pa–pa dair watchin' de stooge on television, you know. An' his pa–pa look at Tijon an' he see dair's somet'ing wrong, an' he say, "Tijon, w'at in de worl' de matter wit' choo?"

He say, "Pa–pa, I got to wrote how–you–call a hessay story on a word de teacher gave me, an' I don't know w'at de hell dem word mean, an' you know how bad I want to be a journalism."

His pa–pa say, "W'at in de worl' is de word?" He say, "Here it is r'at chere F–R–U–G–A–HELL, pronouce 'frugal.' "

His pa–pa say, "It don't mean a damn t'ing excep 't'rifty.' "

Well, Tijon don't know w'at de hell "t'rifty" mean, he in a hell of a fix, you know dat? He walk back in de kitchen an' his older sister was back dair fix some supper, an' she say, "Tijon, you down in de dump, how come?"

He say, "Look, I got to write a t'eme or a t'esis or a hessay, how-you-call a story, on a word w'at de teacher gave me. An' I ax pa–pa w'at de word an he tole me iss anodder word—I don't know w'at de hell bot' word."

She say, "W'at de word?"

"De word is 'frugal,' " Tijon say, "an' I ax pa–pa

an' he tole me 't'rifty' an' I don't know w'at de hell "t'rifty.' "

She say, "It don't mean a damn t'ing 'cept' 'to save.' "

"W'at you said?"

"It don't mean a t'ing in de worl' 'cept' 'to save.' "

He say, "You don't mean to tole me! I'll see you later, I got an idea to write dem t'eme, dem t'esis, how—you—call hessay."

Nex' day he walk hisse'f in school an' he got a han' up w'en he come in dem class. Teacher say, "Tijon, you want somet'in'?"

He say, "Oh, yeah, me, I done wrote a t'eme, a hessay, how—you—call a t'esis, a real story."

She say, "Good?"

"Hell, yeah!"

"You want to read it to de class?"

"R'at now!" An' he pick his paper up like dat an' he say:

"Once upon a time dair was a beautimous fairy female princess lady womans an' she was ride t'rough de fores' wood swamp LOPETY, LOPETY, LOPETY, LOPE on her horsin' back an' she don't know—she ain't got some idea—dat dey been dig a big pit out dair to trap dem animule wit' a tail on bot' en—how—you—call el—e—phant.

"An' she LOPETY, LOPETY, LOPETY, LOPE, KER-SHOOM r'at in one dem hole, an' it kill her horse dead an' she sit on de side of dem horse an' she talk wit' herse'f, "Woe is wit' me, in fac', I got it all over me, I ga—ron—tee. W'at I'm gonna did? I can't got from dis damn place, dis hole too deep.'

"An' about dat time she hear come t'rough dem fores' wood swamp LOPETY, LOPETY, LOPETY an' she

98

say, "Dass somebody, yeah! An' she don't give a damn if he frien', foe or somebody alse.

"So she yell real loud, 'Frugal me! Frugal me!' An' ride t'rough dem fores' wood swamp was one dem charmin' prince on dem white chargin' horse. An' he hear dat 'Frugal me! Frugal Me! Frugal me!' an' he talk wit' his horse, 'Stop you'se'f an' screech to a dead still,' an' she hear dat LOPETY, LOPETY, LOPETY, LOPE stop isse'f, an' she yell sommore, 'Frugal me! Frugal me! Frugal me!' An' he hear dat an' he jomp down off dem white chargin' horse w'at he got, you know, an' he run over dair an' he look down in dat hole an' saw dat beautimous fairy female princess woman lady girl sit dair on her horse, an' she saw him peep over de corner like dat, you know, an' she look upon him wit' bot' eyes an' she yell, 'Frugal me! Frugal me!'

"An' he jomp down in dat hole an' frugaled her an' dey lived happily ever after, I ga—ron—tee!"

Table Manners

You know, not far from where I live—I live dair in sout'eas' Lewisana between Denham Springs an' Franch Settlement—dey got a fallow dair w'at got a whole bunch o' chirren. I t'ink de las' time he count 'em he got t'irteen. An' dey don't got much down dair. Dey trap an' dey fish an' dey raise a garden. Sometime he work, sometime he don't—he don't give a damn, him.

But dey always plant some sugar cane, an' dey make syrup dair, molasses avery year, an' dey got somet'in' to eat all de time, an' dey got a cow give planty milk, an' dey got butter, too. An' I want to tole you peoples somet'in'. If you don't know what soppin' is, you don't know somet'in' none a−tall. I ain' talk about dunk, no. I'm talk about sop. Dair's a big different. You jus' stick dem cornbread or bis−kit down in somet'in'—dass dunk. But sop, you got to motion aroun' a li'l bit.

An' dem chirren—dey don't know nothin' a-tall any some hardly but dem good bis−kit w'at dey ma−ma make. Dey don't bought nothin' but flour, bakin' powder an' coffee—dass all dey got to bought. Dey don't know nothin' but soppin'—put dem good butter on dat an' sop it up wit' dem molasses. Dey can have averyt'in' alse, but dass all dey want to do—dey love dat.

One day dis fallow met up wit' anodder fallow live way away—'bout 10 mile at leas'. He say, "How come you don't drop you'se'f by to see me, hanh?" Well, don't you never ax a Cajun to drop hisse'f by to see you, 'cause he gonna brought hisse'f r'at now.

An' dey were dair one Sunday jus' about to sit down to dinner, here come dat man wit' his whole fambly. "Ho," he say, "I'm glad fo' you to see me, I ga−ron−tee."

Dat odder Cajun say, "I'm glad fo' you to see me, too. Brought you'se'f in de house an' we gonna have some Sunday dinner r'at now."

Iss de same t'ing. When dey got in dair de ma−ma tole dem chirren, "Look, you be on you' bes' behave, you year? Don't you cuss at de table or anyt'in' like dat." Well, dey sit down dair an' she got a boy dass about 12 or 11 year old—big, tall boy—an' he reach over wit' his knife an' put it in de butter an BLOOM! she hit his han' wit' her knife an' mos' broke de knife.

He yell "Whut in de worl' de matter, ma−ma? How come you hit me like dat, hanh?"

She say, "How many time I tol' you, lick you' knife befo' you put it back in dem butter, hanh?"

100

Smaht Cajun

I got a frien' an' he got one boy chirren dat finish high school, an' he smaht enuf where he can go to college. An' somebody tole dis frien' wit' me—he live quite a piece from L.U.S. dair in Bat—onh Rouge, mus' be mos' t'irty mile—he tole him about dat good school in Bat—onh Rouge. An' he mortgage averyt'in' w'at he got to sen' his boy to school dair.

He don't got some money to brought hisse'f home avery week, even dough iss jus' t'irty mile. An' also too he don't want him to mess up—he want him to go ahead an' learn how to be somet'in' in de school. But his son wrote him a postcard an' tol' him he's gonna brought hisse'f home fo' Christmas an' w'at day he was gonna be dair. An' MANH, dat Cajun got in his pirogue boat an' WHOO, up an' down de bayou. Tol' dem, "My boy gonna brought hisse'f home. I want all you all dair to meet him. We gonna bubbercue averyt'in', we gonna have a sauce piquante, a jumble—laya, averyt'in' you like we gonna have down dair—brought you'se'f."

An' w'en his son got home dair must have been 100 or 99 peoples dair to meet him. An' his proud pa—pa say, "Son, brought hisse'f here. We so proud fo' you to see us, an' we proud wit' you at L.U.S. learn to did somet'in' wit' you'se'f. Would you please tole us somet'in' you learn up dair?"

Well, de boy jus' been dair long enuf to be ambarrass. He say, "Pa—pa, you jus' don't go an' say somet'in' w'at you learn up dair."

He say, "Look, boy, w'at you took up dair. W'at kine of schoolin' you took?"

"Pa—pa, I took algebra."

"Hokay, son, say somet'in' in algebra r'at now."

"Oh, pa—pa, I can't did dat."

An' his pa—pa say, about to have an apologetic strokin', "Look, boy, I done spen' my las' money w'at I got on you fo' you to got some educate, an' here you come tole me you can't said somet'in' in algebra. You better said somet'in', or you won't be able to go back to school no time. I'm gonna beat yo' head from you."

De son say, "Hokay, pa—pa. Pi R square."

His pa—pa look at him an' say, "Now if dat ain't a damn fool. Averybody know pie are roun'—cornbread are square."

Talking Dog

Not long ago a Cajun walk into de ol' Sazerac Bar in New Or—lee—anh an' he had dis lickin' pot houn' wit' him name Fido—dey spell dat P–H–I–D–E–A–U–X. He walk in dair wit' dat dorg an' dat bar—tendin' peoples say, "Got dat dorg out o' here. We don' 'low no dorg in de Sazerac Bar."

Ma' frien' say, "Hol' you'se'f still. Dass a differunt kine o' dorg."

He say, "Look like any ol' ordinary lickin' pot houn' to me."

Ma' frien' say, "You don't unnerstan'. Dis dorg can talk."

An' dat bartendin' peoples say, "Look, peoples come in here all de time tryin' to got a drink fo' free. You know dat dorg can't talk."

He say, "I know dat dorg CAN talk, an' I don't want a drink."

He say, "W'at you want, hanh?"

"I want a beer."

He say, "Hokay, I'm gonna give you a beer, an' dat dorg better talk."

He say, "Hokay, Fido, jomp on dem stool." Ol' Fido jomp on dem stool an' jus' sit dair, you know.

He say, "Gimme my beer," an' de bartendin' peoples gave him his beer an' he drank it down. He say, "Fido, I want you to tole dis ol' bartendin' peoples w'at dat is up dair." An' he point to de ceilin'. "W'at dat is up dair, hanh?"

An' Fido raise his eyeball an' look up dair, look at dat bartendin' peoples an' he say, "Roof, roof."

Dat bartendin' peoples say, "Got out o' here!"

Ma' frien' say, "Wait jus' a minute. He can said somet'ing alse."

De bartendin' peoples say, "He better talk dis time, I can tole you r'at now. If he don't, I'm gonna t'row you an' him all de way across dat banquette into de gotter."

Ma' frien' say, "Gimme anodder beer." An' after he drank it he say, "Fido, I want you to tole dis ol' disbelievin' bartendin' peoples who is de greates' baseball player of all time?"

Fido sit dair an' he t'ought fo' a minute real hard. Den he look up at dat bartendin' peoples an' he say, "Roof. Roof." Manh, he t'rew him out o' dair, an' as Fido pick hisse'f up he say, "What'd I say wrong? Was it Willie Mays, hanh?"

Not Quite Ready

You know, avery once in a while one dem Cajun down dair will see de light—an' I want you to know I'm castin' no aspirations on any religion, I'm for 'em all—get de call an' start to preach. An' dey pretty good, too. Dey don't go to no seminar, dey jus' start to preach. Dey don't have no church, so dey preach anywhere dey can. An' dey got a li'l P. A. system mount in dey car an' dey go to a parkin' lot in a shoppin' santa.

I never will fo'got, one of dem in Denham Springs, where I live, had a crowd of about 40 or 35 peoples an' he was goin' to town—doin' real good. Avery once in a while he was gettin' a good "Amen!" or "Dass r'at!" or "Yeah, Yeah, Amen!"

An' he warm hisse'f up in high gear throttle an' he say, "Averybody want to go to Heaven, I know dat." An' he point his finger at dat crowd an' he say, "All you dair dat want to go to Heaven, step over here by my auromobile." An' all of 'em step over dair 'cept one. An' dis preachin' man look over dair an' say, "Don't you want to go to Heaven, hanh?"

"Hell yeah."

"Well, den, how come you didn't step over here w'en I asked all dat wanted to go to Heaven to brought deyse'fs over here?"

He say, "Well, I t'ought you was takin' a bus load r'at now."

Insubordination

In World War Twice dey got a Cajun w'at went into de sarvice, an' he smaht like hell. He know dat de knowledge o' de boat an' de coas' line from Miami, Florida to Brownsville, Taxes, dat dem Cajun have made him have a damn good chance of bein' sent back to de Golf Coas' near home.

So he enlis' in dair an' dey sen' him back w'en he got t'rough wit' his boot trainin', sen' him to Biloxi, Mississippi, where durin' World War Twice dey had a big outfit w'at search fo' dem submarine in de Golf—an' dey had a lot o' dem down dair, too. So he got dair an' de firs' peoples he see is a chief patty officer from Sout'wes' Lewisana who's anodder Cajun.

Dat fallow say, "You t'rough wit' you' basic trainin', hanh?"

"Hell, yeah."

But dat chief patty officer say, "You jus' TINK you t'rough wit' it. Dair's a couple o' t'ings you ain't learn yet, an' I got to taught 'em to you, an' I want to did dat so you can got t'rough."

"Well, I want to got t'rough. Jus' hurry up."

"Hokay. Less meet tonight out dair where dey got dem big searchin' light w'at look fo' dem submarine, an' you gonna got t'rough wit' you' boot trainin' tonight."

"W'at time?"

"Tan o'clock. Be dair."

"I'll be dair. Don't worry some none a—tall. I'll be dair."

Well, he was dair, an' de chief patty officer say, "Hokay, you gonna got t'rough wit' boot trainin' now. You see dat big searchin' light dair?" SHOO. He turn it on, an' you could see t'ree mile out in Mississippi Soun'.

He say, "Hell, yeah, dair ain't no way to miss dat."

"Hokay, I want you to clam' out on de light, walk out dair on dat beam 'bout half way, turn you'se'f around' an' brought you'se'f back."

"I ain't gonna did dat."

SHOO. He turn de light off an' he say, "You mean to tole me you gonna pass some argue wit' me, you' superior?"

"Dass r'at."

SHOO. He turn de light on. He say, "Don't argue wit' me, no. Walk out dair about halfway on dat beam an' turn you'se'f aroun' an' brought you'se'f back."

"I can't did dat."

SHOO. Turn de light off. He say, "I ain't gonna was'e 'lactricity w'en I'm out chere wit' chew. You realize I can court martial you, hanh?"

"Dass r'at."

SHOO. Turn de light back on. He say, "Don't argue sommore. How come you don't wanna walk out dair?"

"'Cause if I brought ma'se'f about half way, you'll turn dat damn t'ing off."

Hard To Catch

Not long ago I was sit ma'se'f at dat how—you—call revolver bar at de Monteleone Hotel in New Or—lee—anh an' a polli—tician frien' o' mine brought hiss'f in dair dronk—an' good. Now dem stool at dat circle bar move deyse'f slow, slow, slow, go 'roun' 'bout two feets avery minute, an' dis polli—tician frien' o' mine stood hisse'f longside o' me an' commence to make hisse'f a speech. W'en he look up after a minute my stool done move about two feets, an' me wit' it.

Dis fallow look a li'l sopprise, but he move hisse'f over an' got hisse'f close to me ag'in. He commence make sommore talk, an' w'en he look up ag'in I done move anodder two feets. Dis time he los' his patience, plum'. He say, "Juice—tanh, hol' you'se'f still, manh! How you 'spec' me to make spoke wit' you w'en you keep movin' away, hanh?"

Impulsive Farmer

Las' week a Cajun come runnin' up to me an' he say, "You know somet'in', Juice—tanh? I got to quit drinkin' like dat, I ga—ron—tee."

I say, "W'at de trouble, manh? Dass fun. You got to relack you'se'f so you won't took you'se'f too serial. W'at happen?"

He say, "You know, I jomp on my tractor de odder day—jomp on it backwards. An' I unploughed over 100 acre befo' I realize w'at I was doin'."

Backward Cook

Saveral year ago I was in a little town in Sout'wes' Lewisana in one dem small hotel w'at sarve breakfas', an' if you come in you gonna got de same t'ing—you jus' tole 'em w'at you want.

I was sittin' in dair an' a man come in an WHOO! I've seen some hang-aroun's in ma' life, but dis has to be de king size. De one he had on was de wors' or de bes' one—I don't know which—dat I never saw befo' ag'in in ma' life, I ga—ron—tee. You could took his pulse from six foots, an' you could reach out an' feel de air, CHOOM, CHOOM, CHOOM, CHOOM. He walk in dair an' he kinda ease hisse'f into a chair 'cause he don't want to hurt dat chair. An' dat waiter brought hisse'f over an' say, "Ma' frien', how would you like you' eggs today, hanh?"

De fallow look at de waitin' man wit' bleedshoot eye an' he say, "Liminate dem egg, please. Jus' 'liminate dem egg."

De waitin' man say, "W'at you said?"

107

"I said 'liminate dem egg." He say, "Hokay," an'
he brought hisse'f to de kitchen. Soon he's back dair wit'
some ham an' scramble egg.

De costomer cas' one bleedshoot eye on dat, an' he
say, mad like anyt'ing, "Didn't I tole you to 'liminate
dem egg, hanh?"

An' de waitin' man say, "I tole dat damn ole cook
back dair, but she don't know nothin' but fry an'
scramble, I ga—ron—tee."

Suspicious Character

Years ago in de Cajun country dey had dese
sellin' peoples—drummers—who would come dair.
Today we still got in de bayou w'at like a school bus, but
it ain't. Iss a general sto' on wheel goin' down de bayou.
An' dese peddlers dat would come dair, dey had de same
route dat dey travel all de time.

I never will fo'got one of 'em. He wen' way back dair
in de marsh—all de way, plum', where de peoples hadn't
been out to de highlan' in all dey life. An' he was down
dair one day an' he stopped at a man's house. He had all
kind o' stuff on his wagon, an' de man came out an' say,
"Well, dair ain't no use fo' you to stop here 'cause ma' ol'
lady ain't here."

"Well," he say, "you can look. I'm gonna have to go
up de road an' aroun' de curve an' all. I'm gonna have to
brought ma'se'f back. W'en she's back, mebbe you got
some money."

De man say, "Mebbe so, mebbe so."

So he look t'rough de wagon, an' he fine a
mirror—lookin' glass—an' he never saw one befo' ag'in
in his life. An' he pick dat up an' look at it. He look at it

108

de secon' time—did one dem triple take, you know. An' he talk wit' hisse'f, "Well, w'at you know about dat! A pitcher of my ol' pa—pa. I got to have dat," he say. "How much you want fo' dis?"

Well, don't worry, Dat peddlin' man done read his mine. He heard him talk wit' hisse'f. He say, "Five dollar."

De man say, "Jus' a minute, an' he go back in de house go look in de sugar bowl underneat' de sugar. He know his ol' lady got $5 hidden dair. An' she don't know dat he know she got it. So he drop dat sugar in a cup, take de $5 out dat sugar in de sugar bowl, go back out an' buy dat pitcher of his pa—pa. WHOO BOY! He so proud, WHEE MANH! Den his face took isse'f a fall w'en he t'ought, "If ma' ol' lady know I took her money dat she don't know I know she got, she goin' stomp me. So de bes' t'ing fo' me to do is hide dis in de barn, an' r'at now!"

So he go out to de barn—he got some hay out dair—an' he look at dat pitcher, he say, "Oh, pa—pa, I'm so glad to have a pitcher wit' you." An' he put it underneat' dat hay an' come on back to de house. His ol' lady is off to a neighbor house durin' dis time helpin' somebody deliver a baby—somet'ing like dat—an' she came back. She didn't notice her money gone, but she spy him go out to de barn avery now an' den.

She say, "Whuss wrong wit' him?" He was so nice—too nice, you know how it is. An' she check dat sugar bowl an' de money's gone. But she don't know dat he knew about de money, an' she did not want him to know dat she knew dat he knew, you know. Iss gettin' dark an' she watch him run out dair to dat barn, an' he light a lantern while he's out dair. After jus' a li'l while he turn dat lantern off SHOOM, an' brought hisse'f back to de house.

She say, "Now I'm gonna wait 'til dat ol' goat's asleep, an' I'm gonna go fine out w'at de hell he got hid out dair in dat barn," 'cause she done put her eye to de crack dair an' watch him go underneat' dat hay pile.

So she wait 'til he asleep an' she light dat lantern an' she go out dair, an' she hol' dat lantern up high an' she look in de haypile an' she scratch aroun' all underneat' dair where he had been lookin' at de mirror an' de pitcher of his pa—pa. An' she reach in dair an' grab dat mirror an' pull it out an' look at it, hole it up at avery angle where she can got a good look.

She say, "Well! So dat's dat ol' hussy he been runnin' aroun' wit'."

Instant Knighthood

Durin' World War Twice I never will fo'got, dey hauled off an' induced me at Camp Beauregard at Alexandria. An' w'en dey did dat dair was a flock of odder Cajun got induce at de same time. Dey couldn't spoke good Anglish, like me, an' in fack quite a few o' dem could not speak a word o' Anglish a—tall, any.

One time we lef' Camp Beauregard an' we got in a troop train to be transfer somewhere in Taxes after we got in—speck an' examinate by dem harmy doc—tor. One li'l fallow name Broussard couldn't spoke Anglish, an' at dat time I spoke pretty good Franch.

Two day later we got to Camp Walter, Taxes, an' w'en we got dair we was unload . . . wit' not a uniform fit anybody. Dey line us up an' here come a shavetail—dat's a 90-day wonder—a secon' lieutenant. He step hisse'f up to me an' he say, "Whuss you' name?" An' I tole him, "Juice—tanh Wilson, sir." So he wrote it down real good. Nex' to me was dis li'l bitty short Cajun Broussard, an' de shavetail say, "Whuss you' name?" An' he say, "Hanh?" He don't unnerstan' nottin'.

De lieutenant repeat hisse'f, "Whuss you' name?" An' Broussard say, "Hanh?"

So I whisper to him in Franch to tell him de name. He say, "Broussard."

An' de lieutenant snap, "Say SIR."

An' dat Cajun say, "SIR BROUSSARD."

Bushy–Tailed Be–Be

I wanna tole you one my favorite story. It happen a long time ago w'en chirren used to walk to school—dass been a long time ago fo' sho. Out in de country in a li'l small town dair was a li'l boy name Henri—dass in French. In Anglish iss Henry.

Henri jus' start to school de firs' year, an' one day he brought hisse'f home from school an' go into de back yard an' look fo' his ma–ma over dem wash pot where she belong— an' she not dair, no. So like all li'l chirren—it make no different where dey from—he start to yell, "Ma–ma, where you at, ma–ma, hanh?"

An' she answer him from inside de house, say, "Henri, I'm inside de house. Shot up all dat yellin' out dair an' brought you'se'f in de house."

He say, "W'at de matter, ma–ma, you sick, HANH?"

She say, "Didn't you hear me tole you to shot up all dat yellin' an' brought you'se'f in de house? Me, I'm not sick, no."

So Henri brought hisse'f in de house an' saw his ma–ma sat up in de bed. He say, "Ma–ma, I t'ought you tole me you was not sick?"

She say, "I'm not sick no, Henri."

He say, "Whut in de worl' you dues up on de middle o' de bed like dat, hanh?"

She say, "I got a new be—be, Henri."

She turn de cover back an' she's nursin' a bran' new be—be. He say, "You don't mean to tole me!"

She say, "Dass r'at." He say, "Well, where in de worl' did you got him, ma—ma?"

She say, "Out dair in de wood in a hollow stump."

He say, "How you like dat! W'at you gonna did wit' him, ma—ma?"

She say, "I'm gonna nurse him an' raise him to be a big fine boy like you, Henri."

He say, "Ma—ma, you reckon if I wen' out dair in de wood an' look in a ole hollow stump I might fine me a be—be like dat, hanh?"

An' she kinda grinned—she wanted to got rid of him anyhow—an' she say, "I reckon you might did dat, Henri."

SHOOM. Into dem wood. Henri look in a very hollow stump he can brought hisse'f to, but he don't fine no be—be, no. He about to give hisse'f up an' he t'ought about one more hollow stump a mile from his house where he can got dair an' look an' got to his house befo' dark. An' he go look in one more hollow stump. An' dair's a great big albino possum soun' wit' sleep.

Henri say, "Look at dat! I done foun' me a be—be, I ga—ron—tee! An he reach down an' pick dat ol' possum up an' put it to his breas'—an' de ol' possum played dead. An' Henri jus' start runnin' to his house, lovin' an' pettin' an' pattin' an' kissin' an caressin' dat be—be w'at he foun'. "M—m—m—m, you cute li'l t'ing . . . WHOO WHOO MANH, ma—ma gonna be jealous of me 'cause her be—be ain't cute as you—I know fo' sho'." He jus' lovin' an' kissin' an pettin' dat be−be all de way. "M−m−m−m, de neighbors ain't gonna like us 'cause none o' dem got chirren cute like him, ho, ho! You cute li'l t'ing, you."

An' 'bout half way home dat ol' possum got tired o' all dat lovin' an' kissin' an' caressin' an' pettin' an' pattin', an' he brought hisse'f out o' dat ball. An' w'en he do he latch onto Henri r'at dair—grab him in his ches', an' good! An' Henri bawl an' squeal an' holler an' bellow, him, but he don't let go of his be−be, no. He jus' run toward his house fas' as he can, an' meet a full−grown man. An' dat man say, "Henri, w'at you got dair?"

He say, "Oooh, oooh, oooh, I got a be−be, ooh, ooh, ooh, dass w'at I got r'at dair."

De man say, "You don't mean to tole me!"

Henri say, "I ga−ron−tee, ooh, ooh, ooh."

De man say, "Where in de worl' did you got dat be−be?"

"Ooh, ooh, ooh, in a stump, a hollow stump. Dass where I fine dat be−be. He's mine, ooh, ooh, ooh."

"Well," de man say, "W'at you t'ought you gonna do wit' dat be−be?"

Henri say, "I'm gonna wean him if he aver turn me loose!"

Ask a Silly Question . . .

You know, lady an' gentlemans, dis Cajun was ridin' along by one dem new plant w'at dey built along de Mississippi River dair in river Cajun country, an' he got trouble wit' his auromobile. Dey got a big shop dair—look like a meck−a−nick shop, an' he walk in dair an' dair's one meck−a−nick workin' in dair, an' he can see he work on heavy equipment. He don't want him to mess wit' his auromobile.

So he say, "Ma' frien', could I use you' foam, hanh?"

De man say, "Yeah, r'at dair on dem desk is a foam."

Well, he go over dair an' look at dem foam, an' it got saven or six o' dem li'l but—tonh on dair w'at you punch, an' he can tole dey got a switchin' board. So he holler at dem meck—a—nick, "Ma frien', how you got outside, hanh?"

An' dat Cajun say, "Me, I use dat door r'at back dair."

Acid Test

At L.U.S., where I wen' to school fo' five year an' I would still be a frashman if I brought ma'se'f back, we got a pretty good football team. An' las' year a whole bunch dem reportin' peoples—de press an' TV peoples an' radio peoples—was talk wit' de coach about w'at kine of team dey gonna have. "Oh," he say, "we gonna be pretty good."

But you know how dem coach are. Dey can't tole you nothin', dey 'fraid to.

An' one dem reportin' fallow say, "W'at you mean, 'pretty good?' "

"Well," he say, "iss gonna be 'bout average dair, we may lose half de game."

"You know you ain't."

"Well, mebbe we gonna win 'em all."

So dem reportin' peoples wrote a story in dey notebook, an' all o' dem lef ' 'cept one—he lef ', but he

114

brought hisse'f r'at back. He say, "Coach, look now, I know you fo' a long time. We . . . "

"Oh," de coach say, "hell, yeah, we frien', dass r'at."

He say, "Look, now, you done tole us all dis stuff, an I know you gonna have a good team. Dis is off de record. I got to fine out somet'ing. You got to tole me. How do you get all dis good material which you get here at L.U.S., hanh?"

"Oh," he say, "you know how it is. We jus' scout dem school dair an' sign 'em up an' t'ings like dat."

He say, "Look, dat ain't how it is. I know dat, coach. An' I ga−ron−tee, on my word of hon−or, I will not tole somebody not none a−tall, won't wrote a story, won't mention a t'ing about it. But please tole me how you got all dem big fine strong boy w'at you got in dat line. I would like to know."

De coach say, "You swear you won't tole somebody?"

"Manh, I ga−ron−tee I won't tole somebody."

He say, "Hokay. W'at we dues, we go out in de country, ride down dem country road an' we look fo' somebody w'at plowin' a mule or maybe two mule—we still got place like dat in Lewisana, you know, where dey plow dem mule." He say, "We fine' one an' we see him go an' down dem row—big fine country boy dair. Den we pull ou'se'f to a dead still. An' w'en he got to de turn row on de end where we at, we ax him how you got somewhere, 'can you tole us how to got to dis place?' An' he was show us an' we sign him up."

Dat newspepper people say, "You mean to tole me dat jus' because he can tole you how to got someplace you sign him up?"

An' de coach say, "Only if he point wit' de plow, I ga−ron−tee."

115

Out of the Habit

I got a couple o' friens'—I don't aver tell any religious stories to refleck on anybody, but I belong to five o' dem an' I jus' go along anyhow—I got a couple o' friens' dat live down in deep Sout' Lewisana dat are priests. An' dey live in adjoinin' parishes, r'at close, but dey don't never got to see each odder 'cause dey so busy. An' dey talk on de foam all de time, an' one day dey was talkin' wit' each odder an' one o' dem say, "You know, I'm so busy I jus' don't know w'at to did."

De odder one say, "An' me, I ga—ron—tee."

De firs' one say, "Look, how come we don't took a vacation, hanh?"

"Say, I never t'ought about dat, me. Less did dat."

So dey arrange to meet each odder at New Or—lee—anh Hinternational Arrowport. Dey got dair an' put on a sport shirt, an' dey got one dem jet plane CHEE—YO, Los An—ge—lees, Hollywood, but dey don't stay dair, no. Dey jus' change plane, got on anudder jet plane CHEE—YO, Hon—o—lu—lu, OH BOY! An' dey go down on Waikiki Beach to a big hotels w'at dey got dair, an' dey don't got a room, no. Dey got a whole damn suits, wit' fou' or t'ree room in dair.

Den dey go down to de basement o' dem hotel. Dey got shop all aroun' where you can bought somet'in', an' dey see one dem shop w'at sell all dem loud clothe w'at peoples wear on Waikiki Beach. An' dey got—bot' of 'em, each one—got a loud shirt an' a pair o' short w'at look jus' like drawer, you know.

An' dey go out on Waikiki Beach one day an' lay up dair, an' dey drink up dem sunshine, discuss all de problem w'at dey got. But de maines' t'ing is, dey relack demse'ves. An' here come a blond female girl lady

116

woman WHOO BOY! in one dem peek—i—nee bathin' suit an' she walk by dair an' dey put bot' eyeball on her r'at quick. She say, "Good mornin', Father. Good mornin', Father."

An' I want you to know dat kinda took 'em from behin'—somebody recognize you so easy like dat.

Well, dey go back to dem same shop in de basement o' dem hotel, an' dey say, "Look, you got to sol' us somet'in' much mo' louder den w'at you done sol' us. In fac', we want de mos' loudes' shirt an' short w'at you got." An' dey sol' 'em de mos' loudes' shirt an' li'l drawer w'at dey got—in fac', dey so loud you can hear 'em long befo' you can see 'em, I ga—ron—tee.

An' dey go back out dair nex' day on Waikiki Beach an' dey lay up dair an' dey drink up dem sunshine WHOO BOY, discussin' all dey problem w'at dey got. But de maines' t'ing is, dey relack deyse'f.

An' here come dat blonde female girl lady woman WHOO BOY, in one dem peek—i—nee bathin' suit, an' dey put bot' eyeball on her r'at now, an' she walk herse'f by an' she say, "Good mornin', Father. Good mornin', Father."

One of 'em say, "Hol' you'se'f still. Dat's true we pries', an' we proud we pries', but how in de worl' did you recognize us so easy like dat, HANH? Would you mine tole us how you could see t'rough our disguise, please? If you don't, it gonna worry us to deat'. Please tole us, hanh?"

She say, "You mean to tole me you don't recognize me? I'm Sister Theresa."

Direction Finder

Down in Sout' Lewisana is a li'l town name Iota, an' iss jus' like iss name—about dat big. An' I never

117

will fo'got, I got to brought ma'se'f to Iota, an' I can't fine dat place, no. An' I'm so los' I don't know where I'm los' from, an' dass bad.

An' I see a fallow walkin' along an' I brought ma'se'f to a dead still an' I say, "Brought you'se'f here, ma' frien', I want to ax you somet'in'."

"W'at dat is?"

"Can you tole me how to got to Iota, hanh?"

"Iota?"

"Dass r'at."

He say, "Lessee, dis road w'at you got r'at cheer, don't leave dat. Go down dair to de crossin' road an' w'en you got dair took a lef' han' an' go two mile an' a half, den took a r'at han' an' go—an' fine a place to turn you'se'f aroun' an' brought you'se'f back here—dat ain't de way to go, no. Less see, Iota."

I say, "Dass r'at."

He say, "Like I'm tole you, w'en you got to de crossin' road you took a r'at han' an' go two mile an' a ha'f, an' took a r'at han' an' fine a big driveway an' turn you'se'f aroun' an' brought you'se'f r'at back here. Dat ain't de way too, no."

He say, "You got to go to Iota?"

"Hell, yeah!"

"Well," he say, "you can't got dair from here, I ga—ron—tee."

Supernatural Dock

You know, down in Sout' Lewisana we try to teach our chirren how to hont w'en dey real young, an' I got a frien' w'at got a li'l boy chirren not quite tan, an' he

118

tol' him one day, he say, "Son, iss time you learn how to hont dem dock, an' I'm gonna get de vary bes' to show you how dass did, an' dass me. But it don't did some good to fine dem dock if you don't know how to shoot dat, an' I'm gonna got de vary bes' shot to show you how dass did, too—an' dass me. An' tomorrow mornin' we goin' out to got dem dock."

He say, "Hokay, pa—pa."

Well, nex' mornin' dey go out an' dey got in de pirogue boat, you know, an' dey go to de blin', an' de ol' man stake bot' side of dat pirogue boat out in case somebody shoot straight up. An' you better did dat, 'cause if you don't KA—SHOOM, she gonna turn over. An' he tol' his li'l boy peoples, he say, "Sit you'se'f down dair an' be quiet. W'en some o' dem dock come close I'm gonna call 'em in an' put 'em down in front. I'm gonna show you how to shot wit' dat twice—barrel Caribbean w'at I got."

Not long befo' here come two dock by deyse'f an' de ol' man called em up, QUANH, QUANH, QUANH, QUANH, QUANH, an' he put 'em r'at down in front, you know, an' he raise his twice—barrel Caribbean an' go KERBLOOM, KERBLOOM an' dem dock jus' raise deyse'f up an' fly off.

He say, "Son, you jus' don't know, you, how glad, me, I am dat you brought you'se'f wit' me today, I ga—ron—tee, I ga—ron—tee! Ho! Some peoples live to be 110 an' don't got to see w'at you, a little bitty peoples not quite tan, already saw today. Mos' peoples live all dey lives an' don't got to see a miracle an' here you, a little bitty boy peoples, already see a miracle today."

De li'l boy say, "W'at miracles you talk about, hanh, pa—pa?"

"W'at miracles I'm talk about? I'm talk about de miracles of dem two dead dock got up an' fly like dat!"

119

Crack Shot

I got a frien' w'at miss one dock season—firs' time in 20—odd year. He been have de same guide all de time an' he fo'got—missin' dem year—dat guide had a bad failin' fault. An' he had brought hisse'f down to go hontin' wit' him an' dey glad to see each odder an' got deyse'fs in bed in dat houseboat so dey can got up in de mornin' an' put deyse'fs in dat pirogue boat.

Ma' frien' got hisse'f up, open his bag an' he fo'gct dat one failin' fault w'at dat guide got, an' dat is dat he can't resis' dronk all de whiskey in sight CHOOM! ISS GONE W'EN HE SEE IT! So he put a fif' of whiskey out dair—Bourbon whiskey—an' dat guide eyeball SHOOM, and latch onto it r'at now.

He say "How 'bout a drink?" Well, dat dock honter still don't remember, an' he say "Hokay." De guide got dem bottle an' he got a deat' grip on dat an' he don't let go.

He han' his coffee bottle to ma' frien' an' say, "You took dis. I'll brought de whiskey." Dey got in de pirogue boat an' he was sippin' along dair on de whiskey. He got to de blin' an' de dock don't come too close. But dat guy he try to call a few—QUANH, QUANH, QUANH, QUANH, QUANH. He didn't got 'em close, but he drank avery bit o' dat whiskey, an' he got so dronk he got to lie down in de pirogue boat—an' dass bad. An' ma' frien' drink all dat coffee, an' it don't help him none a-tall.

Dey make a decide dey might jus' as well brought deyse'fs back home an' de guide's dronk an' here come a dock one in a bunch all by hisse'f. An' ma' frien' call him—QUANH, QUANH, QUANH, QUANH, QUANH—an' he brought him up close an' he got his ah—romatic shootgun an' lifted dat t'ing BLOOM, BLOOM, BLOOM,

BLOOM, BLOOM—an' don't move one feather. An' dat dronk guide raise up wit' his one—hole single-barrel Caribbean BLOOM . . . SHOO! Kill dat dock dead. Ma' frien' say, "I want to tole you, dass a damm good shoot."

De guide say, "I don't t'ought iss so damm good. I should of got 12 or 11 out of a bunch dat big."

Drastic Measures

Dis fallow make hisse'f a batch o' corn whiskey, an' he meet anodder Cajun on de street an' he offer him a drink out o' his jug. He say, "Took a drink out o' dat. See how you like it."

"No, man, I don't want none o' dat, no."

"Oh go ahead, took a drink. It ain't gonna hurt you none."

"No, I don't want none, some, any."

So dis fallow drag a .45 out of his pock—ett an' shove it r'at in his face. He say, "Took a drink, an' r'at now."

De odder fallow say, "You know, you jus' convince me." An' he go GLUB, GLUB, GLUB, an' he mos' choke on dat stuff.

Den the firs' one han' dis fallow de gun an' say, "Now hol' dat gun on me an' make me took one."

Dronk Driver

Near Bat—onh Rouge we got a bran' new four—lane highway, an' dis fallow was drivin' on dat four—lane highway an' he wasn't 'zactly dronk. He was jus' took all four lane an' bot' shoulder, KEEBLOOM,

KEEBLOOM, KEEBLOOM. An' r'at behin' him was one dem preachin' peoples, you know, an' he's concern about dat fallow took all four lane an' bot' shoulder, KERBLOOM, KERBLOOM, KERBLOOM. An' he concern too 'cause he can't got by him.

Well, dat dronk lit his cigaret an' dat car straighten isse'f up an' dat preachin' peoples ZOOM wen' r'at by him, an' he watch him t'rough de behin' view mirror. He watch him real good, in fac' he watch him too good. De road turn, but preachin' man don't. BLOOM. He run upon one dem lovely live oak we got down dair an' tear his auromobile up, plum'. An' dat dronk drove up, brought hisse'f to a dead still, reach down an' pull his immer—gency broke so de car won't roll, struggle out and jus' as he did dat de preachin' peoples struggle out too, an' de dronk say, "Hurt, ma' frien', hanh?" De preachin' man say, "No, not a scratch." WHOO BOY, de dronk tole him wit' a big breathe o' relief, "You lucky, yeah, to tear you' auromobile up like dat plum' an' don't got a scratchin'. You jus' don't got some idea how lucky you are, no."

An' de preacher say, "No, ma' frien', I'm not lucky, me. De Lord was wit' me in dem auromobile."

An' dat dronk say, "De way you drive you better let Him ride wit' me, 'cause if you don't you gonna kill Him."

Fire an' Brimstone

You know, lady an' gentlemans, one preacher down dair in Sout' Lewisana, whenever a new fambly brought isse'f into de community, he always go call on dem. An' he been live dair all his life, an' he love dat

122

Lewisana hot sauce, green an' red pepper an' Tabasco an' pepper sauce. An' he notice dese peoples w'at he goin' to visit dair brought deyse'fs from way up Nort', an' he brought his own hot stuff wit' him an' dey set de meal out dair.

He put some on his food dair, an' dis young fallow wit' his pa—pa an' ma—ma he say, "We better go along wit' him," an' he put some jus' like de preacher dues on his food an' dey eat, but it was too strong.

An' dat young fallow can't stood it, he say, "Preacher, I wanna ax you somet'ing." De preacher say, "Well, go ahead, ma' son."

De young fallow say, "You preach hellfire an' brimstone an' damnation an' all dat, hanh?" De preacher say, "I t'ought dass ma' duty to do dat to show peoples whuss gonna happen to dem."

An' de boy say, "Well, I've heard dat all ma' life, but you're de firs' preacher I ever saw dat took his samples along wit' him, I ga—ron—tee!"

Unsociable

You know, in Sout' Lewisana we got a h'oil company w'at did a shook—up wit' dey personnel becaus' dey got to change de way dey operate. Dey got personnel w'at been wit' dem fo' a long time—25 year an' two day—an' dey don't want to lost dat. W'at dey want to did is to keep dem good personnel, an' got rid dem bad.

Dey don't know w'at dey gonna did wit' de Cajun, 'cause dey don't spoke English—not much, anyhow, not good like me. An' I never will forgot, dey got two mens work togedder from de day dey been wit' dem h'oil company. Well, dey didn't want to lose dem, dey good

123

men, so dey sen' 'em to de foreign country call Awk—la—homa, an' dey sent 'em togedder so dey got somebody to talk to—each odder.

Dey go to work in one dem big pumpin' station, you know. An' dat pumpin' station got a park w'at got a bull wheel 18 feets long—big t'ing. An' one day dey brought dey'se'ves to work dair an' one dem Cajun say, "Manh, I'm gonna go make out de report." Well, dass a lie. He gonna make out he make out de report—he don't know how to wrote nuttin'. An' de odder say, "Me, I'm gonna put some h'oil on dem wheel, an' r'at now."

Well, he got one dem blue danyum jomper on, you know, an' he didn't button de sleeve. An' he go to put dem oil on de wheel an' de wheel jus' reach out an' got him, KERBLONH, KERBLONH, KERBLONH. An' his frien' hear dat man's KERBLONH, KERBLONH, an' he run to de door to see his frien' go KERBLONH, KERBLONH. He jus' watch him go KERBLONH, KERBLONH, KERBLONH. An' dat blue danyum jomper it don't hol' wit' dem wheel too good, an' after awhile it loose isse'f an' BLOOMH, up against de wall it chunk dat Cajun—knock him plum'.

An' his frien' run over dair to see him an' he's shakin' an' he say, "Speak wit' me. You know you ain't dead, no!" But he didn't say one word. So he shook him sommore an' say, "Speak wit' me, I can't stood dis." He didn't say a word. He say, "Look, don't lef' me in dis foreign country smack dab by ma'se'f, no! Spoke wit' me!" An' dat Cajun open one eye an' look at him, you know. He say, "You see, you ain't dead! Spoke wit' me, an' r'at now!"

Dis fallow cass one eye on him an' he say, "Spoke wit' you? How come I should spoke wit' you? I pass ma'se'f by 20 time jus' a while ago, an' you did not spoke to me one time."

Indecent Exposure

Not long ago in Bat—onh Rouge de police got a call from an ol' maid female lady, an' she say, "Brought you'se'f, an' quick!"

Dey say, "How come?"

She say, "Dair's a man nex' do' to ma' house wit' indecent exposin' hisse'f, an' I don't like dat some a-tall."

So dey sen' one dem petroleum car r'at now wit' de syringe on full blas'. W'en dey got dair de policemans knock knock on de do', an' de ol' maid female lady answer de do' an' she say, "Brought you'se'f wit' me." He follow her into de bedroom an' she point nex' do' an' she say, "Look at dat! Don't dat a shame? A man exposin' hisse'f to a maiden female lady woman like me!" An' de policemans look over dair an' dair is a man in his bat'room window shavin' hisse'f, an' he got one dem high window which hit him r'at about at de shoulder, you know.

He say, "Lady, look, I can't took dat mans downtown fo' indecent exposin' hisse'f. All I can see is his head, neck an' shoulder. I can't took him downtown fo' dat."

She say, "Stan' up on one dem box over here, an' you'll got a much mo' better view, I'll ga—ron—tee you dat!"

Old Shell Game

Dis fallow brought hisse'f to de country sto', an' he say like dis, "You got some egg, hanh?" "But fo'

125

sho'," de man say. "De vary bes' Lobell farm egg fo' 40 cent a dozen, dem."

Noticin' a few crack egg, de costomer ax like dis, "How much fo' dem crack egg, hanh?" "Well," de man say, "we got a few crack over dair, an' w'en we got a dozen we sol' dat for' 15 cents."

"Hokay," de costomer say, "crack me a dozen, an' r'at now."

Mule Power

I got a frien' w'at live across de river from Bat—onh Rouge near Port Allen, an' he got de fines' garden you never saw befo' in you' life. Iss fo' or t'ree acre, an' iss a wondermous garden. If a blade of grass is on dair, it belong dair, you year?

One day one dem Cajun come by dat don't care 'bout nothin', an' ma' frien' say, "Would you like to see my garden? Iss absolutely beautimous."

Dat Cajun say, "Me, I don't care one way or de odder."

So he show him aroun' an' he ax him, "How you like ma' garden, hanh?" He say, "Oh, pretty good."

"Pretty good, hell," ma' frien' say. "Dass one de vary bes' garden you never saw befo' ag'in in you' life."

Dat Cajun say, "Look, I can show you how you can improve it 100 percent." He say, "Dair ain't no way." He say, "Oh, yes dair is. Jus' got you'se'f a white mule to plough dat garden wit', an' you ah'romatic improve dis garden 100 percent."

Ma' frien' say, "A white mule?" He say, "Dass r'at." Ma' frien' say, "Got out o' here. You jus' tryin' to put me hot, an' you done did it."

126

Well, he lef', but he done plant de seed, you year? WHOO! "Plow ma' garden wit' a white mule. Improve it 100 percent. He done los' his feeble mind. But I got to plow it anyhow. I might jus' as well plow it wit' a white mule. I got a frien' wit' me between Fordoche an' New Roads got a white mule an' dey bot' retire. I'm gonna go see if he won't sold him to me."

So he go dair an' he say, "Look, I'd like to buy dat ole white mule you got dair."

He say, "Oh, no, I could not sold him. He like a member of de fambly. We gonna retire toget'er."

"I was gonna give you $150."

"You done got you'se'f a mule."

Ma' frien' say, "Well, I can't took him home today, but I'm gonna brought ma'se'f back tomorrow wit' my pickin' up truck (dass a country Cadillac) an' ma' trailin'. But I want to pay you r'at now."

He say, "You don't got to pay me . . . "

Ma' frien' say, "Oh, yes I do. I'm gonna play bourre tonight an' I may not have a nickel tomorrow."

He say, "Hokay." An' SHOO, SHOO, SHOO, he give him t'ree $50 bills.

Nex' day he come back in his pickin' up truck an' his trailin', an' dat fallow met him at de gate. He say, "You know dat white mule you bought from me?"

He say, "Of cou'se I know him. I put my money."

"Well," he say, "It broke ma' heart to tole you dis, but las' night he haul off an' drop dead, an' I done been to town wit' de money you give me an' bought some dat good Cajun whiskey, made in Tennessee, Jacques Dan—yell, some pop wit' foam on top an' a few good clothes, an' I ain't got no money lef'."

"Dass bad," ma' frien' say. "But how 'bout help me load dat ol' dead mule in ma' trailin' truck?"

He say, "Whut in de worl' you gonna did wit' a dead mule?"

"I'm gonna raffle him off, dass w'at I'm gonna did."

"A dead mule?"

He say, "Hell, yeah, jus' he'p me put him in de truck."

"Hokay, I'll he'p you, but I ain't gonna have no part of dem raffle."

"Hokay, you ain't gonna have no part of dem raffle."

So he he'p him load de dead mule on de truck, an' he don't see him fo' about fo' or t'ree week. An' he run into him an' say, "Did you raffle dat ol' dead mule off?"

He say, "You doggone r'at I did. I sold 1,000 tickets, $1 a chance. I made $250 less de cost fo' print de ticket."

He say, "Manh, I bet you made a lot of people hot on de collar."

"Only one—an' I gave him his money back."

Yardsticks

De odder day I was goin' from Denham Springs, where I live, to Dead of Island, an' had an appointment wit' a real good frien' o' mine name Alma Picou, a real fine Cajun lady. W'en I got down dair in a vacant lot r'at nex' to Alma's combination barroom—saloon, cocktail loonge, an' dance flo', dair was a whole bunch of Cajun got a—hol' o' one dem telephone pole, 17 or 16 of 'em got dat pole dair holdin' it up. It wasn't in de groun', no, but sittin' dair wit' de big en' up in de air. An' sittin' on top dat big en' was a li'l bitty Cajun wit' a tape measure in his han' tryin' to got somebody to caught it, you know.

An' like a fool I say, "W'at y'all doin' dair, hanh?" An' dat li'l bitty Cajun cass an eye on me an' say, "Any fool can see w'at we're doin'. We're tryin' to measure how high dis pole is."

I say, "Lay it down on de groun'. You can measure how long it is easy like dat."

He say, "We KNOW how long it is. We want to fine out how HIGH it is."

Durable

One time I went to Prairieville—I got a good frien' over dair got a sawin' mill, you know. An' I got dair about 4:30 o'clock in de evenin' an' dass pop time—pop wit' foam on top. Ma' frien' was dair an' we was jus' fixin' to have one w'en here come a li'l boy about 11 or 10 year ol'—cute li'l boy.

An' ma' frien' say, "Whut can I did fo' you, son?"

De li'l boy say, "Pa—pa want 57 four—by—twos."

Ma' frien' say, "How long you want em, hanh?

An' de li'l boy say, "Me, I don't know."

"Den go back home an' see how long he wants 'em. I'll wait cheer fo' you."

"Hokay," de boy say, an' he lef' his wagon dair an' it took him about an hour to brought hisse'f back.

Ma' frien' say, "Now you can tole me how long you' pa—pa want dem 57 four—by—twos?"

An' de li'l boy say, "He gonna buil' a house. He want 'em a long, long time."

Misfit

Dis frien' wit' me brought hisse'f by a shoe shop in Loff—i—yette an' ax de soldsman fo' "a pair o' dem black shoe in de window numbair 'laven." De soldsman look t'rough de shelf an' tol' de costomer, "I only got it in tan in you' size."

"Look here, ma' frien," de costomer say, "how you 'spec' me to wear a ten w'en I ax you for' 'laven?"

Cajun Praise—i—dent

You know, I got some frien's hang deyse'fs out in de barroom saloon, an' one dem fallow say, "We ought to get us a Cajun for praise—i—dent, us."

"W'at you talk?" anodder say. "We a'retty got us seven Cajun Praise—i—ent, an' dey sure mess up averyt'in'. Dair was dat fallow got us in World War Once name Boudreaux Wilson, an' dat mans w'at r'ar back an' pass a depressin' name Hebert Hoover, an' dat rough—ridin' Thibodaux Roosevelt w'at carry a big stick, an' de praise—i—dent w'at insult a noospepperman w'at talk about his daughter, Harry Trahan, an' dat Francois Roosevelt w'at put averybody in welfare, an' den dair was Lyndon B. Jeansonne w'at want to give away de country an' police de worl'. An' finally we got us Reechard M. Nix—onh w'at gave us de waterbug. No sir, dem Cajun Praise—i—dent done us enuf damage a'retty, dem."

Phony Recipe

Dey got dis fallow in Sout' Lewisana w'at plant hisse'f de bigges' cornfiel' you aver cass an eye on, an' one day he spied a crow fly isse'f aroun' in dat cornfiel' an' BLOOM BLOOM, he kill dat crow daid.

Now dis pa'tic'lar crow had been banded by de Washington Biological Survey to check de immigration habit o' de bird, an' de farmer fine a ban' on his laig wit' how—you—call 'breviate like dis: WASH. BIOL. SURV.

De nex' week de farmer make talk wit' a frien' w'at he got an' tole him 'bout dat banded crow w'at he shot in his fiel'. An' his frien' say, "W'at you did wit' dat crow, hanh?"

"Jus' like de instruc's say," de farmer tole him. "I wash him, biol him an' surv him, an' he still taste like de devil, I ga—ron—tee!"

Home Reducin' Plan

Down in New Or—lee—anh at de conclude of Jackson Avenue an' Prytania Street was de office of a reducin' parlor where dey sol' dem machine gonna brought you' weigh down wit' how—you—call mass—age. Out in de fron' is a big sign read HOME REDUCING PLAN.

Well, a fallow name Bordelon brought hisse'f in dair, an' he say to de soldsman like dis: "Ma' frien', I got a big cu—rous to fine out if I can reduce de note on ma' house w'at I got from $60 to $50 a mont'. You can tole me how I'm gonna did dat, hanh?"

Wrong Dock

Dis young lady from New Or—lee—anh study dat good Franch at dem Too—lane University, an' one mornin' she was squat in a dock blin' in Sout'wes' Lewisana an' she say to her Cajun guide like dis: "*Quelle heure est—il?*"

De guide scratch his head an' he say, "Lady, dem wasn't teal, dem was mallard."

Expansion

After a big flood down in a Sout'wes' Lewisana town dis ol' fallow got his house mess up, an' good, from de water stoodin' in dair for four—tree day. After de water recede isse'f some young fallow from de neighborhood brought deyse'fs dair to help clean up de place. When dey finish clean up de debris one dem young fallow say to de ol' man w'at own de house, "Would you like us to put some paint inside here, hanh?" An' he say, "Hell, yeah!

"Less paint it white," one dem young fallow say. "Make it look bigger."

An' de ol' man say, "You know, I could use more room."

Dead Giveaway

Dey got a hont guide w'at got a beautimous dog, an' w'en one dem city slicker come dair to make some hont he say to de guide, "Dat dog hont dove?"

De guide say, "No,"

"He hont duck?"

"No."

"Whass he good fo' den?" de city slicker say.

"Quail," de guide say. "He's de fines' quail hunter w'at you never saw befo' in you' life. W'en he come to a dead still an' point, dair got to be a quail dair, I ga—ron—tee."

So dey go out in de wood an' firs' t'ing you know dat dog tail got stiff as a bo'd, an' he raise his fron' paw an' point in de bush. But jus' as he do dat a li'l boy rise up from dat bush an' start to walk hisse'f away.

"Dat boy don't look like no quail to me, no," de city slicker say.

"Well, he mus' got a quail in his pock—ett, I ga—ron—tee you dat," de guide say. Den he call to de boy, "Son, brought you'se'f here."

De li'l fallow come over an' de guide say, "You got a quail in you pock—ett, hanh?"

"I don't got no quail in my pock—ett," the li'l fallow say.

"You jus' help you' pa—pa clean out de quail cages, hanh?"

"We don't got no quail cage."

"Well, den, you had quail fo' breakfas'?"

"Ain't taste no quail fo' six mont'."

De guide scratch his head, an' he say, "W'at you' name, son?"

An' de li'l fallow say, "Bob White."